Malcolm has lived for, prayed for, worked for, [...]
thirty years. This book is the fruit of his quest [...] [...]
spark to ignite the fire of revival in your heart, your church, your community and your nation. The most exciting book on renewal in a generation.
Simon Ponsonby, St Aldate's, Oxford

Malcolm Macdonald masterfully draws God's living water from our ancient wells. Not just to give his readers a quick drink, but with his charism as a giant of faith, to raise our ambition. What does it mean to be 'saturated by God' in a way that transforms lives, churches, communities and society? I loved it!
Jill Duff, Bishop of Lancaster

A realistic assessment of where we are and a hopeful portrayal of where we could be. We are praying with Malcolm for the move of God he writes about so clearly here. Might we see floods of revival again.
Gavin & Anne Calver, CEO, Evangelical Alliance & Unleashed Overseer

We are taught to have ears to hear what the Spirit is saying to the churches. Malcolm Macdonald has done that and captured it wonderfully in this book. It is a word for our time as he calls us back to the Church's roots in the presence and power of the Holy Spirit and encourages us to prepare for the revival future God has for us. Sharp analysis of the state of the Church today deeply convicted me about the poverty of my life in God and yet I was filled with hope as I read of past revivals. This book invites us to believe for more of God.
Revd Canon John McGinley, Leader of Myriad

Saturated with God echoes the cry of many hearts in the church today; 'there must be more than this'. In a world that has experienced global chaos and trauma over the last few years, this book provides fresh hope and life for those seeking more. Malcolm provides for us a clear guide to going deeper into both God's presence and God's power; one that he has consistently modelled personally in his own life and ministry. I highly recommend it.
Nicola Neal, CEO, Every Life

Saturated with God is not just a good book. It is a very good book. It is a 'must-read' book for ministers and church leaders. It is informative about historic revival in the Church. It is inspirational in the way it lifts your heart heavenwards. It is instructive in that it is practical and enables each of us to know how we can pursue more of God in our lives, churches and communities. What I find helpful is the way it moves seamlessly from scriptural exegesis to historical illustration to offering food for the soul. It's an easy read, but it's also a deep read. It's a resource for ministers who wish to teach on the realities of revival, the place of prayer, and what scripture has to say about these things. The chapter titles and subtitles themselves are an inspiration: 'lost world' and 'dry Church', 'communities transformed', 'power from heaven'. But at the same time, this is not in any way triumphalist – and throughout the book, particularly in chapter fourteen, the cost of embracing a commitment to revival is spelt out. If this book does not encourage you to pray for more of God's presence in his Church and world, you need to see a doctor!
Revd Canon John Dunnett, Director of Strategy and Operations, Church of England Evangelical Council (CEEC)

Though his style is contemporary, Malcolm's writing reminds me of classics from old-time revivalists – the names Leonard Ravenhill, A. W. Tozer and Duncan Campbell come to mind. Indeed, the author quotes from Campbell, and illustrates from the Lewis revival Campbell took part in, recurrently. But he doesn't just reiterate what these divines have previously written; rather he shares from the holy discontentment and passion of his own heart. That longing for personal and corporate revival is the heartbeat of this study – a palpable yearning that is truly uncommon in the twenty-first century western Church. Malcolm offers a sobering diagnosis of Church and state. His prognosis is to highlight the need for holiness of lifestyle and ongoing, heart-felt 'knee business' (prayer). Combined with a sense of humility – regularly admitting his own inadequacies – and sprinkled with numerous testimonies, both from his own life and that of his Essex fellowship, this book will surely serve to deeply challenge and stir the heart of every reader who loves the Lord. As Malcolm opines; 'If Jesus is at the centre of everything, revival will (surely) come'.
Tom Lennie, Revival historian, and author of three historical studies on Scottish revivals: *Glory in the Glen, Land of Many Revivals,* and *Scotland Ablaze.*

SATURATED WITH GOD

SATURATED WITH GOD

A cry for a nation-changing revival

Malcolm Macdonald

First published in 2023
by SPCK

First published in Great Britain in 2023

Society for Promoting Christian Knowledge
RH101, The Record Hall
16 16A Baldwin's Gardens
London EC1N 7RJ

British Library Cataloguing-in-Publication Data
A catalogue record for this book is available from the British Library

ISBN 978-0-281-08803-4
eBook ISBN 978-0-281-08804-1

1 3 5 7 9 10 8 6 4 2

Typeset by Fakenham Prepress Solutions, Fakenham, Norfolk NR21 8NL
eBook by Fakenham Prepress Solutions, Fakenham, Norfolk NR21 8NL
First printed in Great Britain by Clays Ltd

For my parents,
John and Liz Macdonald.

You were the first to show me
a God-saturated life.

Acknowledgements

I really just have one sermon that I have shared everywhere for the last 30 years: *revival*!

This is my second book, but just like my first one, it also comes from my one sermon.

As with *Set Me on Fire* (Monarch, 2015), the backdrop has been an early morning Bible teaching series at New Wine in 2018 called *The Missing Revival*, plus our local church vision statement, *Every Person, Every Place, Saturated with God*, which means the book will be grounded both in biblical teaching and in local church practice.

I am very grateful to New Wine for giving me the opportunity to teach this, and also to share it on New Wine Online. Caroline and I have found a home in New Wine for over 20 years now and love being part of such a movement seeking to see local churches changing nations. That is what we are all about.

I also want to honour my church family at St Mary's Loughton. We have served there since 2009. They have had to put up with my 'one sermon' for all those years. God has called us to serve and we are grateful to be part of this amazing community. This book is a summary of our church vision, and I feel so blessed to be able to try to live it out each day there.

My real joy is my family. They put up with me more than anyone and I love them so much. Thank you, Caroline, not only for being such an outstanding partner in the gospel, but for being such a remarkable wife. My kids are such a blessing and I love them more than I can say. Beth, Lucy and Joshua – as ever, I pray you will all go much further than me in knowing Jesus.

Finally, my sincere thanks to the team at SPCK. People don't realise what goes into publishing Christian books. This team are genuinely amazing and do a great job. Thank you all for all your help, advice and support.

This book has been in my heart for years. I write to ignite others around me. I write for you, with the heart that God will meet with you more powerfully than ever before. My hope and prayer is that someone will pick up this book and be transformed and go on to see revival.

Contents

Contents

Foreword

How much of God can we have? How much of God do we *want*?

These two questions go right to the heart of discipleship. They speak of whether we are truly surrendered to God, and of whether we have discovered that he alone can satisfy and that his presence is worth paying any price to obtain. As Jesus said in the famous parables of the Hidden Treasure and the Pearl of Great Price – such simple stories that together take up only three verses of Matthew 13, and yet still so challenging – the experience of the Kingdom of God here on earth cannot be matched by anything else this world can offer. This book will awaken a deep desire for this Kingdom in you, or – if it isn't something to which you can relate to at this point in your walk with the Lord – I believe that it will *create* this desire in many.

We live in a society that too often celebrates playing it safe. When you're interviewing people for jobs, occasionally you will see someone referred to as 'measured'. At its best, and appropriately so for certain roles, this can mean that the individual is calm, doesn't act rashly or disproportionately, and isn't subject to unpredictable and dramatic gestures. But what can be a virtue in some pursuits is a serious failing when it comes to our relationship with God. We cannot take a 'measured' approach to loving him and seeking more of his power and presence in our lives.

Perhaps we fear excess or are concerned about creating a sense of 'hype' that carries people away on an emotional wave that is simply manipulated or manufactured. But that is far less of an issue than we make out. As the former Bishop of Coventry, Cuthbert Bardsley, said in the 1960s, 'The chief danger of the Anglican church is not delirious emotionalism'. We might add, 'Nor in most other churches'. God deserves and demands our all, so our worship cannot be anything other than with the our whole heart, soul, mind and strength. Far from that being a barrier to the gospel, something that turns others away from our faith, the world is looking for a Church that believes what it preaches. In fact, the world today demands passion rather than caution. The measured approach often masks complacency, comfort and compromise.

Not only is God worthy of all our passion, but he has himself has acted with passion towards us. Whenever we think of loving him, we must realise that he loved us first. Whenever we challenge ourselves to pursue him, let's never forget for how long he has pursued us. Whenever anything in the Christian life feels like 'sacrifice', we need to call to mind his complete self-giving on the cross. Truly, we cannot outgive God.

So, to return to the questions we began with: How much of God can we have? How much of God do we *want*? God never creates a deep desire in us that he is not willing to satisfy. It says in John 3.34 that, 'God gives the Spirit without limit' (NIV) – or, 'by measure' (KJV, RSV and others). There is no holding back on God's side. He is looking only for people who desire to receive him, not only for themselves but for their communities. As Malcolm sets out so wonderfully in these pages, God's plan of salvation and redemption leads to a new creation where his presence and glory fills all things. Graciously, that future reality has broken into human history, at least in part, on numerous occasions, giving us a glimpse of the glorious reality of heaven to come.

A powerful movement of God is long overdue in these lands. It is happening today in many parts of the world, but few if any in the UK can recall such days of people being swept up in the power and presence of God. Malcolm has had the privilege of hearing first-hand from some of the surviving witnesses to such moves of the Spirit, and it has formed and shaped him. I know, from years of close association with him, that he is paying the price in yearning for the next great awakening – searching the scriptures, learning what it is to be saturated with God's presence, pressing into his wonderful promises. And I have seen God use him to spark the same desire in others.

How much of God can we have? As much as we want. Dare we believe it?

Paul Harcourt, New Wine

Introduction

Water is such a simple part of daily life, we barely even stop to think about it. It is so basic to human existence. Every day we need to drink and rehydrate. We all need to drink to live. Everyone knows how utterly essential it is for life.

Water is also a powerful image in Scripture. Even today, it's part of our shared language of spiritual growth, discipleship and revival. We talk about feeling 'spiritually dry' or praying for an 'outpouring' of the Spirit. We believe in being 'baptised' in water and we speak of suffering as 'passing through the waters'. Water is deeply emblematic of a Spirit-filled life.

The image of water is a deep deposit of biblical reflection and also contemporary Church longing. It flows throughout Genesis to Revelation in many forms to describe human life and give expressive language to describe our encounters with God. It is copiously used in Scripture, songs, prayers, prophetic words and teaching in the Church today. Given all that, I wonder whether we have fully explored this teaching and language in the way God intends us to?

When I wrote *Set Me on Fire* in 2015, I wrote about the image of fire through Scripture, such as with the burning bush in Exodus and Pentecost in Acts. Now, I want to do the same with water. All I can say is that reflecting on this theme of being saturated with God has blown my mind and expanded my heart. As I began to see this in Scripture and also in church life, especially among those who are hungry and thirsty for something more of God in our generation, I started making connections and seeing how being saturated with God was the very heart of discipleship and God's blueprint for revival. God is speaking to us through something as basic as water. He wants to show us his kingdom and it is so basic, simple, real and relevant, yet we are prone to miss it. I pray we can see in these simple images of water how much God wants to send his Spirit in our times.

Since 2016, our local church vision has been *Every Person, Every Place, Saturated with God*. This is our heart and desire. We want to see more people come to faith, everyone loved and cared for, new churches planted, fruitful outreach and mission, and people growing in discipleship; but what underpins us is to be saturated with God. This means encountering God, living for the kingdom, loving deeply and sharing Jesus, but it also means that this only comes through being filled, drenched, soaked and utterly immersed in God himself. I write this with a longing to see revival in my own family, church and community of Loughton and Epping Forest. I want to see genuine revival across the United Kingdom again.

Duncan Campbell described revival as 'a community *saturated with God*'.[1] He led the awakening on the Hebridean Isle of Lewis from 1949 to 1953. I honestly still can't think of a better description of revival and what we urgently need to see in our time. I feel I can see in my heart what God saturating my town might look like and I really want him to come and do it. I see God moving everywhere and his presence coming down on the whole community, not just in the church services. This means many people getting saved, healed, set free, delivered and signs of his kingdom breaking out everywhere. The darkness is pushed back, truth is restored in the public square, cycles of crime are broken, harmful addictions are shattered, emotional healing and restoration increase, justice is advanced and society transformed for every generation. The fear of the Lord renewed in the community and worship and prayer in homes become the best kind of 'new normal'. This is the tip of the iceberg of what I see in my heart as the fruits of a coming move of

---

1   B. H. Edwards, *Revival: A people saturated with God* (Darlington: Evangelical Press, 1990), p. 93; my italics.

God. A coming saturation by God of our nation. A sovereign move of the glorious and life-saturating Holy Spirit.

As a teenager, God gripped my heart with a longing to pray for the UK. I had a small laminated map of Britain in my Bible. I would get it out by my bedside and cry to God for a fresh outpouring. I wanted to see it and be part of the next revival. It was this description of revival as being saturated with God that captured my soul. I began to see it everywhere in the Bible and started to make it my vision.

I feel aware of my soul-thirst pretty much every day. I know how dry my heart becomes when I wander from God in my own strength and in my selfishness. I also know the real difference that being near to God makes, when my life is saturated with him. Once we taste that living water of Jesus, nothing else really satisfies or even comes close. It is this saturating encounter and experience that means we are never the same again. Now, none but Christ can satisfy!

Being saturated with God is my heart's cry. This is how I want to live. It is a compelling vision for life as a follower of Jesus. You can simply pray, 'O God, saturate me with your presence and power.' This thirst isn't inward looking. When I walk around my community I get thirsty for God to move and I feel the spiritual drought all around me. The answer to our barren, spiritually waterless culture and dry Church today is the 'floods', 'rain', 'outpouring' of the Holy Spirit. Our dry and lost world needs the living water of Jesus. Our families, churches, communities need God. They need to be filled to overflowing with God. This is God's answer to our broken and parched world.

Revival is God's answer

I really believe that the answer to the situation that faces us today in Britain is to see a remarkable outpouring of the Spirit across the

Church and nation. I want to be part of a generation that sees a mighty move of God. God's answer is always himself.

We are living in an uncomfortable season. While there are overwhelming and complex challenges facing us, it is also a new season of preparation for a great move of God in our nation and the world. When things seem at their darkest, that is often God's timing to birth something new. This is also a moment for the Church to rediscover kingdom courage and kindness. We live in a perplexing time of hyper-change. It is multilayered and extremely disorientating. Our ethical and moral frameworks have been in free-fall for some time. God would be entirely justified in bringing his just judgement now. But, this is also a gospel-moment of grace. A time of enormous openness and potential for spiritual harvest and revival. Let's not miss this moment, but play our part in prayer and heart preparation for revival.

The time is ripe for revival, if we prepare, repent, surrender to God and pray. This is not a time to be shallow or stick with the familiar and comfortable. The need is so great. As Oswald J. Smith said, 'I know of nothing less than the outpouring of God's Spirit that can meet the situation. Such a revival has transformed scores and hundreds of communities, it can transform ours.'[2] Amen!

Do you have a yearning for personal, regional and even national revival? This book is a call to honestly recognise our spiritual drought and be moved to seek God and be more saturated with the Holy Spirit. Many Christians today have a strong desire for revival and a hunger for something authentic. There are many histories of revivals from the past and also accounts from across the world today, in places such as Iran and China, where revival is happening now. People in the western Church have experienced decline for so long and are aching for something more. This is truer than ever in a post-pandemic world. People realise that this is a moment for the

---

2   O. J. Smith, *The Passion for Souls* (Lakeland: The Chaucer Press, 1983), p. 15.

Church to be flooded again with the love and power of God in a lost and despairing world. We need revival more than ever!

We want to see God saturate our community and we are hungry to see a move of God such as we have never seen before. We want every person to know Jesus Christ and be filled with his Spirit. We want his kingdom of love and power to come in every place. I want to stir up your hunger for God to do something more than we have ever seen before. But, what does that really mean and what would it look like?

Something needs to change for us to see a fresh move of God. What we are currently doing is not cutting through spiritually. Good though it is, we are not yet seeing full breakthrough. If we keep going as we are, nothing new will happen and the revival so often prophesied will never come. We need to learn to drink the living water of Jesus.

As I said, my journey of longing for revival began as a teenager. I gave my life to Jesus at nine years old, and after some time away from the Lord, I was filled with the Spirit at 15 years old as I saw that I was living a compromised, frustrated and defeated Christian life. In answer to a call to holiness and a Spirit-filled life, I went forward for prayer at a Faith Mission conference in Bangor, Northern Ireland, earnestly asking God to cleanse me and fill me with the Holy Spirit, and a real change came into my life. God the Holy Spirit swept in. That night, I stood up to testify to the change God had worked in me at the youth meeting. There were no outward manifestations, but I knew the tangible difference God had made on the inside, which soon showed on the outside.

That day changed my life. It was a deep inward work of the Spirit, a time of personal revival. I came home and started to actually live out my life as a Christian. The Bible became real and alive. I loved our weekly church prayer meeting. I began to encounter God in worship and tasted of his intimate presence. I regularly knelt at my bedside to pray and get into God's Word. I also had a new courage to share Jesus with my friends at school. I didn't care what they thought of me, because Jesus had won my heart.

Around that time, I attended some meetings on the Isle of Skye where I met men and women who had experienced genuine heaven-sent revival. I could never be the same again. Meeting them ruined me for the ordinary. At those meetings I listened to testimonies about the manifest presence of God and I felt his presence there in such power. There seemed to be such a holy longing for God himself to come in power and such a pure love for Jesus in those Christians. It was as if they were describing a different world where God came down in such a real and wonderful way.

The first book I read on revival was *Why Revival Tarries* by Leonard Ravenhill. This was not for the faint-hearted, as Ravenhill called on the Church to stop playing religious games and go much deeper into God in repentance and prayer. This made a real impact on me as a teenager. I loved church, but also could not understand why Christians were so satisfied without the manifest presence of God in their lives, churches or communities.

I listened to hours of revival preaching from Duncan Campbell, A. W. Tozer, W. P. Nicholson, George Verwer and other preachers. I even had a full-size pulpit in my room. I don't know where it came from but I used to preach to myself and write sermons on revival. Put simply, my later teenage years were on fire for God. I started to speak in tongues quite spontaneously one day while at university, a place where I witnessed a wonderful move of God among students. I decided to live all out for God and shared him everywhere. My friends and I started a weekend street outreach and hosted regular prayer meetings which were full of passionate prayer. We used to wait for people to walk along the street, then go up to them to get invited to a party so we could go there to share the gospel with them before we got thrown out. There was a fire in our hearts for prayer, evangelism, holiness and revival. I had a burden for the souls of those around me who did not know Jesus.

Since those fiery student days, I have become a husband, father and church leader. I wish I could say I have had the same energy over the past 30 years since those early days. What I can say is that I have known God's presence through the highs and lows, ups and downs and the pressures of life. Sadly, like many church leaders, I recognise that somehow that thirst wanes when we take on leadership responsibility. Maybe we become too sensible or we too easily settle for the status quo? It is often the burden of maintaining church that drains spiritual life. Many leaders need a fresh touch of the water of life in their souls. Today, I feel a deep desire to be filled as never before. Even though the years can dim our energy, our vision and calling to see God move can increase more and more. Now, the older I get, the more I want to see that genuine move of God in the nation.

Has God planted a seed of longing in your heart to experience revival? My heart is always stirred by people who have tasted something of God's kingdom that is more than I have ever known and that can only be explained in terms of God.

We won't see community transformation through only organising better programmes or improved church techniques, much as I believe these are all necessary. There is a big difference between what we can do and what God can do. God can do immeasurably more than all we ask or imagine. Are we seeing what we can do, or what God can do, today? God is able to do so very much more than we are currently experiencing.

We need to see more of God moving. It's more of God that we need in our communities. More love, more power, more truth, more signs and wonders, more of his presence and peace. We need more of his manifest grace, mercy, joy, hope, healing and holiness in our streets. Revival is not about large church programmes, good services, successful efforts or Christian emotionalism. It is not hype, hysteria or a religious thrill. Arthur Wallis describes it in two simple words: 'God came.'[3] That's it, a visitation of God upon a community. This is what we desperately need today.

I believe it is time for us to get back to the simple gospel of the kingdom. Back to God's Word and Spirit moving together and back to ardent prayer. Are we not tired of the powerless and passionless Church trying to reach our communities in our own strength? The answer is in being saturated with God himself. Imagine your community saturated with God. Ask the Holy Spirit to birth the dream in you of your community saturated with God. People everywhere becoming aware of his presence and being touched by his power. Can you see hundreds and thousands of people coming to Christ because of a deep awareness of his unconditional love and conviction of their sin?

God has given us a dream

Our core Scripture at St Mary's in Loughton is Luke 1.37, that 'nothing is impossible with God'.[4] Gabriel spoke these words to Mary as she heard how God would do something impossible in her to conceive Jesus, the man who is God. Sometimes we just can't fully take in what God can do. Maybe, we don't need to worry about understanding revival and how God does it. We just need to believe, obey and receive what he has promised.

Where is the move of God in our day and our generation? How can we begin to think about actually seeing revival happen? Let's be honest, it seems far-fetched to think of our communities saturated with God, doesn't it? It seems like a dream, something unreal and far away. The brokenness, anxieties and busyness of life press

---

3   A. Wallis, *Rain from Heaven* (London: Hodder & Stoughton, 1979), p. 14.

4   This wording is as in the 1978 and 1984 editions of the NIV; the 2011 edition gives, 'no word from God will ever fail'.

in to cloud such dreams and they all too easily fade. Is that your experience?

May God cause us to dream again of revival. As the songwriter Alex Muir described in his wonderful hymn, 'God Has Given Us a Dream', may we fix our eyes on the glorious days ahead when the light of Christ will fulfil our hearts' desire, where his glory will fill our land. May we see in faith what God has in store for those who seek him.

I have had 'revival dreams' a number of times. They always come with an overwhelming sense of the presence of God. When I dream, I see passionate and packed churches, with people full of God. I see everyday people with a living faith. I see persecution getting stronger, but the Church getting purer and more winsomely faithful to Jesus. This is not a half-hearted Church, but one fully surrendered to Jesus and finding the greater things of the kingdom. The Church I see that is in revival and saturated with God understands the power of the presence of God and is full of repentance, signs and wonders, love and a spiritual thirst for much more than we have ever seen in our land. This Church knows that our God is an awesome God. God has not finished with us yet.

As I write, I want you to meet with God, for you to dream of revival in your life and community. Make space for God as you read. May he cause you to dream of revival in your life, church and community, saturated with himself. May you repent, be cleansed, revived and stirred spiritually as the Lord leads you.

The first part of this book, which focuses on the dry world and dehydrated Church, is painful and expresses a grief for the current state of the Church and the world. The second part is bursting with hope as we explore what being saturated looks like and what the rain of revival might be like. Then finally, in the third part, we turn to what it can look like to be saturated with God in the everyday. What might it look like to live this out?

Get ready to drink, swim, soak and be drenched, immersed, baptised and saturated with God!

Part I

A DEHYDRATED CHURCH IN A PARCHED LAND

Why are we not seeing revival today?

As followers of Jesus, our identity is in being full to overflowing with God himself. Jesus died to win a beautiful Church; his bride, a pure and spotless bride. My heart is filled with a vision of a faithful Church; a Church that loves courageously and is fully devoted to Jesus. Church is the everyday, amazing, diverse people of God from every people, language and nation.

It is because I see this beautiful, victorious and faithful Church, which God intended, that my heart breaks for the Church in the UK today. God intended the Church to be saturated with himself, so it is a tragedy that we are so dry and have so little to offer a spiritually parched world around us. I love the Church passionately, yet also grieve her compromise and dryness.

Can we see that the UK Church is largely not yet what God intended her to be? Many churches are strangers to the Holy Spirit, preach a half-gospel, have no regular prayer meeting, no new converts, no children and youth, no supernatural expectation and no appetite for revival. Some churches could close tomorrow with no visible loss of impact on their community. They are not missed when they close. Heartbreaking!

The first part of this book is painful reading. It is the bad news before the good news. I wish it were not so, but don't we have to be as honest as possible if we are going to change? We need to stir ourselves. Something is tragically missing in many of our churches and it really matters.

Let's start by being honest that we are not (as I write) currently in revival as a Church or nation. There is no use hyping ourselves

3

up. We need to truthfully assess our current perplexing spiritual condition in the UK Church. Put simply, this is not the best God has for us. We are not currently living through a particular high-water mark for spiritual life in the UK.

Where is the revival so many have promised and prophesied is coming? For years, we have comforted ourselves with the thought that revival is just around the corner. And yet, we've not seen a national revival touching all corners of the UK since 1859, when one million people came to faith in Christ across every part of the country. Why are we not seeing such a revival today? We seem so overdue. Where is the missing revival?

Have you noticed something is missing? It actually isn't that hard to spot. Even the world knows things are not quite as they are meant to be. People can see that the Church is not that different from the world around us, but what aches most of all is the lack of spiritual vitality and power to transform communities.

There is an ache in our hearts for much more of God.

I genuinely lament the powerless, fruitless, dry and weary Church across our land today. We are very busy, well organised, expertly managed and are full of creative ideas, so why are we still so spiritually impotent? Why the barrenness? Is this not the elephant in the room in our Sunday gatherings, conferences, Bible studies and small groups? Where is the manifest presence of God? We serve a risen Saviour, but seem so spiritually sleepy. How can this be?

We are seeing lots of blessings and can share great testimonies, for which we are genuinely grateful, but not revival as seen in history and Scripture. It's as if we are content with puddles of blessings rather than rivers of revival.

We have now had decades of charismatic renewal in churches, but our wider communities remain largely untouched by the gospel. Perhaps we really are content with this? We have become easily accustomed to our lack of impact. Proverbs 29.18 says, 'Where there is no vision, the people perish' (KJV). Does this not describe

4

us today? Perhaps we would do better to stop talking about revival being around the corner. Rather, it might be better to be honest and simply lament that we have no revival today. We are not there yet. Then perhaps we might examine why with more vigour.

Has our fire gone out? Has your fire gone out, preacher? Are we content merely with good teaching, decent music, some children's ministry, plenty of church activity, a few minutes of prayer and then some good coffee after the service? Church leaders, don't we want more than maintenance and management for churches? Don't we want more of God!

After these years of renewal, what do we have to show for it of eternal consequence? We have seen some churches renewed, but has our nation or even our community turned to God? Are we even truly evangelical in our clear witness for Christ and love for his Word? Are we honestly charismatic in our demonstration of the gifts and power of the Spirit? Have we become overfamiliar, glazed over and far too bland, boring and predictable? We need to recover prayer, worship, witness and the power of the Word and Spirit. God is bigger than all our church labels and models.

A number of years ago I received this email from a member of the church:

Since joining St Mary's it has felt that we are on the edge of moving into a deeper more powerful and supernatural relationship with Jesus but yet there is something holding us back. It's like we have sold everything to buy that field but cannot seem to find the treasure.

Yes, there is something holding us back. I think lots of churches are in this place. Our years of renewal have been good for lots of individuals, but because we have sometimes been half-hearted, is it not rather disappointing that the nation is still far from God? Where is the fruit? Something is wrong when souls are not being saved.

Don't we want to be in meetings where God breaks through? Meetings where the Holy Spirit actually takes charge. Yet many of our churches are half empty week by week and people are coming less often than ever. Why is there a lack of bright witness, whole-hearted serving, corporate prayer, spiritual power and sacrificial commitment? Maybe some of us don't actually want God to break through?

More than minor amendments are needed. This is not about tweaking. If we are honest we know that currently our churches are powerless to touch the spiritual needs of our communities, because we are trying to do it in our own strength. Our churches are not turning communities upside down with gospel-life as once happened under John Wesley, George Whitefield and William Booth. Sadly, many churches are focused on their own needs first. The consumer church collapses inwards on itself as it only serves itself. We need to own this tragedy and repent.

Our culture is broken and needs the gospel. Sadly, the Church seems impotent so it can't transform the culture. Many Christians are not praying and don't pray with others for a move of God. There is sentiment and fascination about revival, but there is little actual prayer for it. We need a holy discontent with superficial, spoon-fed, consumer church which is filled with activity, but not saturated with God. We have redefined encounter to mean we felt emotionally moved or had a few goose bumps. When we come into direct and living contact with the living, eternal and holy God of the Bible, we simply cannot fail to tremble and be transformed. Our hearts have not yet seen the awfulness of sin, the power of prayer, the majesty and beauty of Christ, the way of the cross or the glorious person of the Holy Spirit. We need more encounters with God, rather than lots of church activity.

It has become normal to accept Christ, but not deny the world. We tolerate sin and are often more anxious about being too radically holy than being sinful. God is our servant. We have reduced him through our unbelief. No longer high and lifted up, we have domesticated him to fit our agendas, requirements and boundaries. Where are the Spirit-saturated disciples who tremble at God's word? People like Moses who had to remove his sandals as he stood on holy ground. What would our Church make of Isaiah's thrice-holy God, before whom he had to sink into the dust of repentance and contrition? God is all love, but not easy-going.

Perhaps the uncomfortable truth is that we are content without revival. The price is too high. Getting right with God is actually not our first priority. We will never get the transformation we long for through programmes, networks, movements, projects, initiatives and such like. We have forgotten that it is, 'Not by might nor by power, but by my Spirit' (Zech. 4.6).

Do we have even one genuine revival leader in the UK today? If we did, we would be currently experiencing revival. Yet, we have no revival. I guess the answer is 'not yet'. Perhaps a life of radical discipleship feels just too much like hard work and something unattainable for us in our relaxed western culture? Can we be 'all in' for Christ and also live in comfort? Is answering this question facing our greatest fear? Is this what is holding us back? Is this what is holding me back?

Let's also be honest that none of us have ever seen revival in this country yet. It's hard to know how to think about all this, because most people don't realise that there is actually much more than what we currently experience.

I feel sincerely conflicted about all this. I am part of the Church I am describing. I have been a Christian since 1985 and ordained for 17 years and I am not as close to God as I want to be, yet also know that so much more is possible. I am not yet as deep in the Spirit as I want to be. My journal is full of phrases such as these:

'I need revival in my life.'
'I need more of God.'

'I need to learn to pray.'
'Why am I not nearer to God?'
'I need to get back to where I was with God.'

The past few years have dented many of us in real ways. There is a profound uncertainty; a depleting sense of insignificance, grief, trauma, fear and confusion that I can see in myself and also many others. A cocktail of soul obstacles that have paralysed the saints. Overall, a deep loss of confidence in what is even possible. Our multiple fears have frozen us and robbed us of hope.

This first part is about a dehydrated Church in a parched land. I said it would be painful, and it is. Not just for other people, but for me. I see myself, my weakness, my sin, my compromise and my part in this season of dehydration; and I lament:

'Lord, have mercy on me.'
'Lord, forgive me as a leader in your Church in this time.'
'Lord Jesus, flood my dry soul with your living water.'

I know I am not great at drinking enough, even just physically. I am not great at hydrating my body. Some people just seem to always have their water bottle nearby and stay fully hydrated all the time. They are the healthier for it! Not me. Why don't I do it? Who knows! It doesn't really make sense, but I just don't. It is a simple reality: not enough water equals dehydration. According to the NHS website, 'Dehydration means your body loses more fluids than you take in. If it's not treated, it can get worse and become a serious problem.'[1]

That is true physically, and also spiritually. If we don't drink in more of Jesus it will become a serious problem. To be spiritually dehydrated is a serious problem. Has the Church lost too much

---

1 https://www.nhs.uk/conditions/dehydration/

water of the Spirit? The revival preacher Robert Murray McCheyne said it this way:

> It is a fearful sign to see so little thirst in you... If the town were in want of water, and thirst was staring every man in the face, would you not meet with one another and consult, and help to dig new wells. Now the town is in want of grace and you yourselves are languishing. Oh! Meet to pray.[2]

When Christine and Peggy Smith, the elderly sisters on the Isle of Lewis, saw there was a dehydrated Church with no young people at all in the churches, they prayed fervently and persistently. For them, really seeing the dryness was part of the route back to living water. When they prayed, God heard and answered with floods on dry ground. Do we know what it is to be truly thirsty? Do we know what it is to be truly saturated?

Over these first three chapters looking more closely at why we are not seeing revival today, may we give some painful space for lamentation, grieving, weeping and honesty and examine our souls in the light of God's Word and Spirit. May we also give space to grace, dreaming, praying, renewal, courage and faith to see who God is and what God wants from his Church. We need to start here, but we won't end here. Nothing is impossible with God and he gets the final say.

---

2 *Sermons of Robert Murray McCheyne* (Edinburgh: Banner of Truth, 2000), p. 16.

1

'A dry and parched land':
lost world

> *You, God, are my God,*
> *earnestly I seek you;*
> *I thirst for you,*
> *my whole being longs for you,*
> *in a dry and parched land*
> *where there is no water.*
> (Psalm 63.1)

Water is the ultimate symbol of life, yet we are living in 'a dry and parched land'. There is a profound challenge here. The psalmist is thirsty for God, but living in a dry and parched land with no water. Part of understanding the need for revival is seeing the incredible need of our local communities and nation as people live without God's living water. We need God more than ever right now. We need to hear a prophetic lament for the missing move of God; the missing revival.

The UK has experienced great outpourings in almost every century over the last 500 years. What about our generation? What about today?

We live in a lost world. More lost than we really know. Have we ever stopped to think just how lost people really are? We easily live and move in a world that is entirely spiritually dry, broken and fallen. It will soon come to judgement and only then will all things be made new. Until then, this world is blindly, painfully and tragically careering towards its eternal destruction. Every single one of the millions of souls in our world was worth Christ dying for and rising again. God loves this world so much. The question is whether we do.

Psalm 63.1 speaks to a longing for God being like thirst in a waterless wilderness. That is exactly what it is like today for everyone who is not yet in Christ. Outside the gospel, there is no spiritual water for those who are thirsty. Without Jesus, there really is no hope, no joy, no forgiveness and no eternal life. Knowing Jesus really is the difference between being spiritually dead or alive.

Where is real hope to be found? What about the promise of enlightenment humanism, the endless possibilities of science, the evolving ideas of socialism, capitalism or liberalism? How is post-modernism or the identity politics experiment doing at creating hope? We seem to live in an increasingly divided, confused, alien-ated, prejudicial and unforgiving time. For all our attempts at making progress and trying to fix the world, humanity only finds itself getting more and more drawn into self-destruction. We seem unable to save ourselves or to really discover anything more than dreaming, wishing and faintly hoping for something better.

Will humanity ever learn that we don't have the capacity to save ourselves? Self-salvation is an arid wilderness. It is a dry and parched land; a waterless, hopeless desert. In our post-Christian world, it seems that the 'self' is the new god our society worships. This is a world that does not even seem to know it is lost. It has become so dry spiritually.

Our world is broken by sin, division, abuse, rebellion and pride. Biblical values have become more offensive than ever to those who have already rejected God. Our politics, media, institutions and culture are all moving further away from their Christian founda-tions. Alongside the very real physical effects of climate change, the world is experiencing an equally real spiritual desertifica-tion. The world is a spiritual wasteland in need of living water to bring new life. People have sadly departed from the one true and available source of meaningful hope: a living relationship with Jesus Christ.

Before the good news can be fully received and have an impact, the bad news needs to be heard and understood clearly. Our sin is breaking us, confusing us, dividing us and destroying us. Do we think we are superior to Noah's generation? The first time God released judgement on the earth in Genesis 6, he used literal water in what we know as Noah's flood. But, we know that the days before the coming final judgement (with fire this time) will be just like the days of Noah (Matt. 24.36–44). The stakes are beyond high. The eternal destiny of billions of people hangs on whether we can grasp this and begin to act.

We have become desensitised to an immoral culture which calls good evil, and evil good. Our culture is lost in lies, self-deception and selfishness. People can't tell their right hand from their left ethically. Judges 21.25 describes our culture perfectly: 'In those days Israel had no king; everyone did as they saw fit.' The Bible eloquently describes our postmodern mindset:

- 'Where there is no revelation, people cast off restraint' (Prov. 29.18 NKJV)
- 'Righteousness exalts a nation, but sin condemns any people' (Prov. 14.34)
- 'Truth is fallen in the street' (Isa. 59.14 NKJV).

Leonard Ravenhill writes:

We need a baptism of honesty in the courts of the Lord. Honesty means truth and truth can be painful. We have not made a dent in the moral corruption of the nations. We are still a valley of dry bones.[1]

---

1 L. Ravenhill, *Revival God's Way* (Minneapolis, MN: Bethany House, 1983), p. 30.

Could this be the low ebb prior to revival? It is true that through history God has chosen the darkest times to pour out his Spirit anew. We sadly live in times of pronounced idolatry, confusion, addiction, promiscuity, division, racism, greed, gluttony, cursing, violence, abuse, unforgiveness, intolerance and fear. I could go on! It can feel overwhelming to contemplate the scale of depravity and suffering in our world.

The bleak religion of self

Our culture is disturbingly self-absorbed, acutely self-sufficient and exalts whatever feels good. 'Do whatever you want as long as it does not harm anyone else.' But, how do we define harming others? Who gets to decide that? What authority do we use to know if harm has been caused?

The cultural shifting we have seen in recent times is described by John Mark Comer in his excellent book, *Live No Lies* (2021), as the 'new religion of self'.[2] Whether it is cancel culture, social media, identity politics or radical individualism, he writes of the Church feeling in a kind of exile in this new culture, saying, 'We're all in Babylon now.'[3] Much of what we can see in this new cultural landscape exists both in the Church and in the world. Sadly, the Church and the world often don't look too different from each other. There is a desire for liberation from what is seen as an old-fashioned moral law and universal authority. Freedom is often seen as actively embracing transgressive behaviour, which itself is seen as in some way more authentic.

This is our post-truth, post-Christian world of mix-and-match pluralism and indifferent agnosticism. We are meant to affirm the self-construction of endless identities with the idea of 'self' placed

2   J. M. Comer, *Live No Lies: Recognize and resist the three enemies that sabotage your peace* (London: Form, 2021), p. 118.

3   Comer, *Live No Lies*, p. xxvii.

firmly at the centre of 'your truth'. This parched path is causing us to drift into an ethical meltdown. Justice, morality, identity and equality have been redefined and twisted into oppression. In a pluralist world of relative morality, the cry is, 'Who are you to judge me?' Yet no one is actually happier.

Ideas have been weaponised, language has been rendered meaningless, tolerance has given way to hostility and truth has been superseded by experience. Media bias is pervasive. Big business and our institutions seem to push ideology. Whom do we trust? Sadly, we seem more divided as a world than ever before.

Some in our society sadly seem to focus on unforgiveness, oppression and rage, not on love, reconciliation and grace. Human-centred ideologies are entrenched in self-deification and have the power to propagate through mobile technology and endless unseen algorithms. Comer writes, 'Over the last few years I've watched so many people, both on the Left and the Right taken captive by ideology. It's grieved my heart. Ideology is a form of idolatry . . . a way to usher in utopia without God.'[4]

Good and evil in society have been confused. Basic Christian ideas like love, sin, justice, equality have all been redefined, misrepresented and distorted in a way that often turns them round a full 180 degrees, to mean the opposite:

Lust is redefined as love. Marriage, not as a covenant of life-long fidelity, but as a contract for personal fulfilment. Divorce, as an act of courage and authenticity, rather than a breaking of vows. The objectification of women's sexuality through porn, as female empowerment. Greed, as responsibility to shareholders. Gross injustice towards factory workers in the developing world, as globalism. Environmental degradation, as progress. Racism, as a past issue. Marxism, as justice . . .

---

4 Comer, *Live No Lies*, p. 38.

abortion, the greatest infanticide in human history is recast as 'reproductive justice'.[5]

All the while the world goes on spinning in its daily cycle of lostness and hurtles towards the day of days when God will judge the earth in righteousness. We have even got to the point now where we think it wise to question whether God is really capable of being just, at least up to our contemporary standards of justice. Shame on us for such arrogance. Any thirst for righteousness is replaced by thirst for happiness, truth is replaced by lived experience and ethics by identity.

Rather than healthy spiritual formation, we are seeing widespread unhealthy ideological formation. This is a postmodern doctrine our children and young people are being expertly discipled in through social media. Is it any surprise that they are leaving our churches at a frightening rate and at the same time we are facing the greatest crisis of mental health, especially in young people, that the world has ever seen? There is a mental health pandemic going on now that is often hidden, but deeply affecting so many people.

We don't know who we really are any more. It isn't real freedom to let us self-select our identity, especially when we are so broken. What a burden! True freedom is discovering our identity in our Creator and Saviour. We don't know how to make sense of this complex, hurting and confusing world and so this has truly become an age of anxiety.

Neither the political right nor left, or centre, seems even remotely equipped to face this world. There is much hand-wringing, but not much hope or any sense of answers from the world. Even those critical of this new religion of self don't themselves know what the answer is to our broken world. They have no real hope to offer. Only the gospel has what it takes.

---

5   Comer, *Live No Lies*, p. 216.

The awfulness of sin

So where do we go from here? It's pretty tough when we get even a small appreciation of how hopeless the world is without Christ. How do we start moving towards hope? I know this is not what we want to do, and it seems counter-intuitive, but if things are going to really change we need to take a long, hard look at the real source, root and ground of the problem; we need to talk about sin.

Our world is lost, dry and spiritually dehydrated because of sin. I know we often want to focus on encouragement, good news and being nice. But if we want to have a better harvest, we need to sow a different seed. Just being nice isn't addressing the real need.

Can we see the world as God sees it? We think the world is a bit messy and troubled, but not so bad. As long as we get our entitlements, holidays, houses, careers, leisure pursuits, Netflix box-set binge and can continue to go about our lives, we don't let the spiritual desert around us bother us too much. We block out the eternal destiny of the people around us to make life bearable for ourselves. Our goal is convenience.

I am calling us to think differently from the start; actually, to think biblically. It isn't a new thought at all. In fact, it is an ancient path and well travelled by leaders in revival throughout history. We need to recover biblical understanding of human sin and our need for a sufficient Saviour from all sin. Over the years, we have downplayed and minimised sin, so that it does not demand so much from us. Only when we have understood or begun to perceive how lost, dry and arid this world is, will we see the glory of God's answer: to be saved and saturated with God. Who cares about being saturated with God unless they know how dry and dead they are without him?

What has been a prominent feature of every true revival? A weighty, necessary, profound and very wholesome conviction of sin. As long as we think we are fine as we are, there will be no need for salvation. Conviction of sin is a central, often undervalued, ministry of the Holy Spirit.

A healthy view of ourselves starts with recognising that God created humanity as 'very good'. Humanity was created in his image; but since the fall of Adam and Eve, we have sinned and been slaves to our sin. The good news of the gospel is that Jesus saves and rescues us from the presence, power and penalty of sin, when we come to him in repentance and faith. An awareness of our sin is essential. It forms the heart of our basic need for God. This is the ground of unconditional and divine mercy, grace and love. Those who know how awful their sin was, know how amazing grace is. We have to talk about sin and how horrific it actually is. Sin keeps us away from God. It separates us from God and twists, distorts and mars our souls. Sin completely destroys us. It is not a frivolous, flippant or light-hearted problem. Sin is literally the gateway to hell; and in Luke 16.19–31, Jesus tells us that hell has neither water nor fire exits!

Let's get into this in more depth. In Romans 1.18—3.20, Paul lays out his foundation for the gospel. A huge component in his teaching was thinking rightly about sin. Why is the gospel good news? It is good news because it is God's rescue plan from the bad news of sin and death. More than that, the gospel is God's kingdom of full salvation coming on earth and into eternity. Paul's teaching in Romans answers the question: how can I have a new relationship with a holy and loving God?

Paul's teaching is about sinners needing salvation, the unrighteous needing the righteousness of Jesus; the lost needing mercy. In Romans 1—3, we see that righteousness is essential, but our sin blocks the way to it. We see the immensity of God's hatred for sin and the wonder of God's mercy to sinners.

How can we find God when we are separated from him through our sin? The truth is that he finds us. Paul starts his gospel with the awfulness of our sin and the just wrath of God against sin! Paul paints an ugly picture of sin. Humanity began with Adam and Eve knowing God, then rejecting God. Humanity thus defied God and sin entered the world. Paul tells us that 'people are without excuse' (Rom. 1.20). These chapters are like a courtroom drama. Paul brings the charges, evidence, cross-examinations, verdict and penalty. It is a trial of the self-righteous and self-obsessed. It is vital to face the truth of the wrath of God against sin. The toxin of sin has spread far wider, faster, more dangerously and more potently than any pandemic the world has ever seen. Sin is deadly. It is perilous and foolish to minimise and ignore it.

A right relationship with God needs right thinking about ourselves and God. We can only really get this understanding by faith in Christ Jesus, and the Holy Spirit revealing this truth to us. This itself is God coming to us in his gracious undeserved favour. This is amazing grace. Jesus makes the first move towards us from heaven to earth. Jesus became incarnate as fully man, already being fully God. He lived a blameless life and then died in our place, for our sins, on the cross, to obtain mercy and forgiveness for us. Jesus came to seek and save the lost (Luke 19.10).

I never get tired of the gospel. It is definitely the greatest story ever told. How did Paul teach the gospel to the early Roman church? He started by recognising human sin. 'There is no one righteous, not even one' (Rom. 3.10). In other words we are all guilty. In Romans 1.29–32, he writes:

> They have become filled with every kind of wickedness, evil, greed and depravity. They are full of envy, murder, strife, deceit and malice. They are gossips, slanderers, God-haters, insolent, arrogant and boastful; they invent ways of doing evil; they disobey their parents; they have no understanding, no fidelity, no love, no mercy. Although they know God's righteous decree that those who do such things deserve

death, they not only continue to do these very things but also approve of those who practise them.

He goes on in Romans 3.11 to say that 'there is no one who understands'. Here we see that sin leaves us in darkness and confusion. In other words, 'their thinking became futile and their foolish hearts were darkened' (Rom. 1.21). Finally, in Romans 3.11, Paul also says that 'there is no one who seeks God'. Everyone is lost. No one is seeking God, not even one! Paul also says, 'They exchanged the truth about God for a lie, and worshipped and served created things rather than the Creator' (Rom. 1.25). Paul goes on, 'they did not think it worthwhile to retain the knowledge of God' (Rom. 1.28) and even describes the effect of sin as making humanity 'God-haters' (Rom. 1.30). This is truly devastatingly bad news. In Ephesians 2.12, Paul describes humanity as existing 'without hope and without God in the world'.

Why do we minimise sin when it separates us from God (Isa. 59.2)? This is bad news, but necessary news, which is why Paul is beginning his teaching on the gospel by focusing on it. We absolutely need to be thoroughly saved, rescued and freed from sin.

Let me ask you, what do you think of sin? Why has sin become so easy to live with when it has caused every war and committed every murder? Sin is the promoter of pornography and sexual perversion. It has perpetuated every injustice and all poverty. Sin is behind every false religion. Sin is the root of all abuse. Sin feeds every alcoholic and addict. Sin is at the heart of materialism and all greed. Sin is the origin of slander, pride, envy, jealousy and hate. Sin is the starting point of climate change, prejudice and hypocrisy. Make no mistake, Jesus hated sin! He came to destroy it. God is holy, all holy, altogether holy, infinitely holy and always holy. Sin is always sinful, all sinful, infinitely sinful and altogether sinful. Our problem is that 'all have sinned and fall short of the glory of God' (Rom. 3.23).

I don't think we have really thought enough about sin as the source of the 'dry and parched land' we inhabit. It isn't complicated, but it is controversial. The very nature of sin means people don't want to hear about it. It is offensive to people to be told they are sinners in need of a Saviour. Jesus told us to expect this reaction to the gospel.

Let me be very clear that the heart of the gospel is God's unconditional love shown on the cross. God loves the world so much (John 3.16). It is impossible to exaggerate the love of God. But, maybe we have sometimes not shared the whole gospel, which also includes being saved from sin, death and hell. Maybe we have done that to make it less embarrassing, but the gospel isn't ours to tinker with or edit. We need to share the whole gospel.

The reason for this is because people need to know not only that they have sinned, but that God's wrath against sin is certain, holy, just and immense. Can we think of God as punishing evil? We can, and we must. The wrath of God is perfect. God's character is not only flawless goodness but also faultless justice. We are prone to regard sin lightly, to gloss over and make excuses for it, but the more we ponder God's hatred of sin and his vengeance upon it, the more we realise its awfulness. Again, let me be very clear. On the cross Jesus delivered us beautifully from God's wrath, but his wrath remains just. Sadly, the subject of divine wrath has become taboo because it offends people. Actually, the Bible is full of God's perfect wrath. John 3.36 reads, 'Whoever believes in the Son has eternal life, but whoever rejects the Son will not see life, for God's wrath remains on them.' Why are we so silent, when the Bible is so vocal?

God's holiness exposes sin and his wrath opposes sin. God does this because he loves us. God will not come to terms with sin. The love and wrath of God burn together in faultless unity. We need to remember that God's wrath is his just, proportionate and holy reaction to evil. It is not a selfish anger or uncontrollable tantrum. God's deep indignation aroused by injustice and sin is a good thing. In his

famous sermon, *Sinners in the Hands of an Angry God*, Jonathan
Edwards said:

> The bow of God's wrath is bent, and the arrow made ready in
> the string. Justice bends the arrow at your heart and strains
> the bow and it is nothing but the love of God that keeps the
> arrow at bay.

So Paul asks, in Romans: if God's wrath is so great, how can we
possibly escape? This is what makes the gospel such a mighty
miracle, such overwhelmingly good news. No sinner seeks God, so
God seeks us in unconditional grace and love. We can be entirely
rescued from sin. There is a wonderful, perfect, sufficient and saturating Saviour from all sin!

When Paul tells us no one is righteous, Jesus makes us righteous
(Rom. 5.1). When Paul tells us that no one understands, Jesus shows
us the Father (John 14.6). When Paul tells us that no one seeks God,
Jesus seeks and saves us (Luke 19.10). I thank God that Jesus said,
'I have not come to call the righteous, but sinners [to repentance]'
(Matt. 9.13). This went on to become a core message of the early
Church as Peter preached, 'Repent, then, and turn to God, so that
your sins may be wiped out' (Acts 3.19), and also John the apostle
promised that, 'If we confess our sins, he is faithful and just and will
forgive us our sins and purify us from all unrighteousness' (1 John
1.9). Despite our awful sin, God first loved us.

Salvation in Christ is about much more than just deliverance
from sin, but it certainly starts there. This is why Jesus had to die on
the cross: to take away our sin and bring us into his kingdom life.
In Romans 3.25–26, Paul goes on to share the power of the cross,
proclaiming that:

> God presented Christ as a sacrifice of atonement, through
> the shedding of his blood – to be received by faith. He

did this to demonstrate his righteousness, because in his forbearance he had left the sins committed beforehand unpunished – he did it to demonstrate his righteousness at the present time, so as to be just and the one who justifies those who have faith in Jesus.

How we need the cross. We need God's mercy, forgiveness and freedom. The whole gospel starts with rescuing us from sin and then extends into God's kingdom breaking through in healing, signs and wonders and miracles. Whole salvation sees God's kingdom coming both now in this world, and then fully in heaven.

So the source of the lostness, dryness and spiritual drought of this world is evidently our sin. We live in a barren wasteland of spiritual need. Things may look OK on the surface, but this parched world has no hope of living water without Jesus Christ, the Saviour of the world.

We started this chapter with Psalm 63 and the longing for water where there was none. Soul-thirst is needed again today. We won't find refreshment in this world, because it is dry. We need to remember that the people all around us who are outside of Christ are living a scorched, thirsty, parched existence. We can only find the living water through Jesus.

2

'Broken cisterns': *dry Church*

> *'My people have committed two sins:*
> *They have forsaken me,*
>   *the spring of living water,*
> *and have dug their own cisterns,*
>   *broken cisterns that cannot hold water.'*
> (Jeremiah 2.13)

I am afraid it gets worse before it gets better. In a spiritually parched world in such need of Christ, we sadly find a dry Church. Jesus gave the Church to the world to show the way to the living water. But tragically, just as Jeremiah wrote of Judah, the Church is itself dehydrated.

It is hard enough that this world is lost without Jesus, but the really uncomfortable truth is that much of the wider Church has engaged in the two sins Jeremiah speaks of: unfaithfulness and self-reliance.

The western Church looks OK, but isn't really. Sadly, we are not ready for revival. That's why we aren't seeing it. We have not yet come to the point of recognising our need for God, repenting and surrendering to Jesus. We see God move in Scripture and history much more than in our contemporary western churches. The Church simply needs to repent. Jesus' last words to the Church on earth were not to 'go', but to 'repent' (Rev. 2.5). We need to humble ourselves before God.

We have become over-sensitised to the world and de-sensitised to the Spirit. Many have a vague sense of Jesus as Saviour, but don't seem ready to submit to him as Lord. This is surely the source of our extraordinary decline in the western Church. It isn't as complicated as some make it out to be. This is why we are not yet ready to be fully saturated and revived.

Again, I believe we have to face reality honestly if we are going to see actual change. I speak as a church leader, hence I can see that so much of our problem is that we have put ourselves at the centre and have become too inward looking. This continues to be a huge problem in the aftermath of the Covid-19 pandemic, which really disorientated the Church.

Much of the contemporary Church wants the benefits of Jesus without any of the cost and commitment. This issue of depth of commitment is huge in the average UK church. It has been eroded even further since the pandemic, with many people simply not returning to active worship, or leaving the Church altogether. Everyone was affected in different ways, and it was really hard. Many churches across the UK experienced a sharp decline.[1] It was a tough time for us all. This was the moment for the Church to rise and shine and touch the nation: we didn't.

Have we learned the spiritual lessons for the Church from the pandemic? Everyone tried to do what they thought best at the time. But I remember being in Zoom conversations with leaders from around the country. The focus was on adapting, not praying. It was about pivoting and a scramble to get on Zoom, Facebook or YouTube, not so much about listening to the Spirit.

One of the key messages I believe we failed to lay hold on in the pandemic was the call to humble ourselves, repent, pray and depend on God. I had a vision of kneeling in front of our church and lifting up my hands towards the community in prayer. The pull

---

1 For more information on national church trends during the pandemic, you can visit the 'Changing Church' survey conducted in autumn 2021 by the Evangelical Alliance at https://www.eauk.org/assets/files/downloads/Changing-Church-Autumn-2021-Research-Report.pdf

to move on with business as usual is very strong. I believe we were sadly often operating in a Covid mindset, not a kingdom mindset.

Times are always challenging. There has been shaking and much discomfort. This is when the Church is called to overflow, because we were designed to be saturated with God and to overflow to others in need. Perhaps this time of dismantling and reformation is what we need in this moment. It could be a place for us to discover that our church culture was somewhat off, even before the pandemic. As Emma Stark pointed out at a conference I attended recently, our direction, emphasis, leaning and ethos often used worldly success measurements and methods. We were more in this world than in the kingdom and have needed a correction season. Our focus was on large 'successful churches', large conferences, celebrity pastors, increasing numbers, big offerings, good media, excellence and professionalism. Our trajectory was off by a mile. It is dangerous to take our eyes off Jesus and put them on ourselves.

This seems like an exile wilderness season for a compromising and powerless Church. A Church where people want to be comfortable will decline via defeat, conflict and carnality. Transformation is costly and takes surrender. God is calling us to be faithful and fruitful, not professional or successful. God will change our measurements from numbers and influence to love and faithfulness. Leonard Ravenhill was right when he declared the biggest threat to the Church was not external, but internal. Our main problem is ourselves, not the world around us. It is the compromise of the Church, not opposition from the world. That is the reason we have no revival.

The wasteland of forsaking Jesus

Could it be that the reason we are a dry Church is that we have forsaken the living water: Jesus? It makes a lot of sense, but is hard to hear. Prophesying for the Lord, Jeremiah laments, 'They have forsaken me, the spring of living water' (Jer. 2.13). We have lost touch with God as our first love. Also, notice that through Jeremiah, God describes himself as 'the spring of living water'. God likens himself to the spring of water! Jesus picked up Jeremiah's picture in Revelation 2.4, calling the Church to repent because 'you have forsaken the love you had at first'. This is a call to return to fidelity, faithfulness, intimacy and passion. To ignore, overlook or disregard Jesus is to invite a wasteland of spiritual dryness. As Bob Conner remarked, 'We have become too casual with a holy God we barely know.'[2]

How central is Jesus to how we actually live and how our churches operate? We want the blessing, but not the lifestyle of Jesus. We want the benefits of his salvation, but not the cost of his lordship. Most western Christians are content with a shallow relationship with Jesus. We know we need him, but are too busy and self-absorbed with life to actually make it happen. When it comes to prayer and being in communication and relationship with God, we have settled for ripples, not rivers. This may not be much better among church leaders. Do we have many prayer-filled preachers today? As Leonard Ravenhill remarked, 'Our poverty in prayer is the seedbed of all our failures . . . There is nothing we need more than a school of prayer. Who dares teach it?'[3]

I honestly think the need of our time is radical repentance, not polite positivity. We should humble ourselves, not congratulate ourselves, and stop protesting our innocence. We alone are responsible for our prayer lives. We cannot blame others for our unfruitfulness as we seem content to remain strangers to God's intimate presence. Our time is similar to that which Haggai spoke into. We have been too busy for God and are preoccupied by doing

---

2 R. T. Kendall, *We've Never Been This Way Before* (Lake Mary, FL: Charisma House, 2020), p. 61.

3 L. Ravenhill, *Revival God's Way* (Minneapolis, MN: Bethany House, 1983), pp. 85–6.

our own thing. When asked his secret of success in ministry, C. H. Spurgeon said, 'Knee work, knee work!'[4]

God have mercy on us for our comfort-driven selfishness, consumerism, devotional superficiality and prayerlessness. I realise this may not be a welcome message for the contemporary Church. I often feel like an outsider in churches when I talk about revival. I am all for open and healthy conversation, dialogue and understanding others, learning and hearing where others are coming from; but we also need to be brave and honest, as the prophets were. We need both conviction and compassion.

Can I say that, as I write, my heart also breaks over my own need? I don't have revival yet in the church I lead. I often lament my own lack of progress into the deep things of God. At a recent New Wine leadership conference, I recommitted myself to becoming a person of prayer. This is what I was born for and what God has called me to, even though it is a struggle. It is hard work. I often fail, I often sadly choose comfort. But, prayer is the only way to fruitfulness. Ravenhill writes:

Many of us have no heart-sickness for the former glory of the church because we have never known what true revival is. We stagnate in the status quo and sleep easy at night while our generation moves swiftly to the eternal night of hell. Shame on us![5]

Perhaps we need to seek urgent spiritual attention for the dangerous symptoms of spiritual dehydration. E. M. Bounds said, 'Men are looking for better methods. God is looking for better men.'[6] If God is convicting you, as he is me, then may we repent and return to our first love: Jesus.

---

4 W. Duewel, *Ablaze for God* (Grand Rapids, MI: Zondervan, 1989), p. 212.

5 Ravenhill, *Revival God's Way*, p. 70.

6 Duewel, *Ablaze for God*, p. 214.

The dryness of self-reliance

Not only has the Church neglected God himself, but we have done things our own way. We have done what we thought was best in our human effort and so the Church has declined in the western world now for many decades. Jeremiah felt this same lament and prophetic burden over his own people.

He goes on to warn the people that they had 'dug their own cisterns, broken cisterns that cannot hold water' (Jer. 2.13). Not only do we forsake our first love, but we find ways to do what we want ourselves, in our own strength. This self-reliance, self-sufficiency and autonomy is the opposite of faith and dependence on God.

Can we see how our ordinary days are often filled with unfaithfulness and self-centredness? This is what God wanted his people to hear through Jeremiah. Do we need to hear it again for our lives?

This is a time to grieve and lament over a broken Church that does not know how to rely on God's power or proclaim the fullness of the gospel any more. Yes, the Church is experiencing trickles of real blessing in many ways, but do you ever feel that something is missing? Why do we see so little of the power of God at work? So much seems to be delivered by human effort, rather than the Spirit's power.

A dehydrated and self-reliant Church is no answer to a lost and parched world. It is not powerful, prophetic or fruitful. It is the kind of Church that society found easy to ignore in the pandemic and see as 'non-essential'. This should grieve us. We were largely laid aside during the pandemic.

We know that the Church did a huge amount, but I am not thinking of it from our point of view; I am trying to see it from the point of view of the world at large. The Church was as powerless as anyone else in those dark days of lockdown. Many of us were just as captive to fear as our unbelieving neighbours. Apart from some excellent community ministry, there was very little difference in the fundamental approach of the Church from secular charities. What kind of Church is emerging from the pandemic? Is it any different as a result? Have we changed? I fear not as much as we might like to imagine.

It's not that there have been no great ministries, blessings or genuine encouragements. Of course, we celebrate every person who comes to faith in Jesus. Each one is precious to God. Each victory is beautiful and I am grateful to have also seen much that has been extraordinary. We are grateful for every healing and every food parcel distributed, every person set free from debt or simply heard in their pain and loved. We rejoice when people are helped practically and loved in any way. We love seeing signs of the kingdom of God. That is what we feel we were made for. But, just as we notice trickles of blessing, can we not also be honest that we also believe the Church was designed for more than a trickle? We were made to be like a roaring river of God's power, love, gospel and life.

Pastor Juan Sanchez describes the seven dangers facing the Church as loveless orthodoxy, fear of suffering, compromise, tolerance of sin, a good reputation, self-doubt and self-sufficiency.[7] Does any of this sound familiar? William Booth's classic prophetic observation looking into the future from the nineteenth century also rings true today. He said, 'The chief danger that confronts the coming century will be religion without the Holy Ghost, Christianity without Christ, forgiveness without repentance, salvation without regeneration, politics without God, heaven without hell.' Are we living in the times he foresaw?

Many western churches are on autopilot – minimising sin, striving for excellence more than purity, marketing more than praying, managing more than repenting, and complying with

---

7   J. Sanchez, *Seven Dangers Facing Your Church* (Epsom: The Good Book Company, 2018).

endless regulations rather than advancing and breaking strongholds. We are sadly often more interested in organising events than in multiplying disciples.

Who cares about the kingdom of God more than their comfort? Oh, for a spiritually vibrant Church looking beyond herself – beyond personal happiness, beautiful homes, personal well-being and lovely holidays. I am honestly writing not to condemn, but to stir us up for much more than we see right now. Stirring vision is uncomfortable. A kingdom vision is always a big vision. It can't originate or grow in a human-centred Church based on human-centred activity, reason and compromise.

A kingdom vision is about loving Jesus more than anything. It has to be genuine love that motivates us. Do we love Jesus more than watching TV, sleep, our phones, spending money as we like, the food we eat, our children, our freedoms and our entitlements? Do we actually live as though we even like Jesus?

Arid compromise

Jeremiah's warning to God's people about forsaking the Lord and living in their own strength was a prophetic challenge to their compromise.

Have you ever gone through the words of Jesus to the seven churches in Revelation 2—3, and noted what Jesus commends and also what he rebukes? I really recommend it, but be prepared to be disturbed as you see your own life and your church highlighted by Jesus. One of the main traits Jesus highlights is churches that are compromising in their teaching or lifestyle.

Instead of living out the powerful truths of Scripture, many churches have adopted a damaging version of identity politics. It is so sad to see the Church reduced in her theology and practice to a tragic version of postmodern, relativist ideology. God's kingdom is one of real justice, peace, healing, compassion, forgiveness and welcome. We don't need the input of human-centred ideologies to grow in discipleship. Jesus is all we need.

Instead of compromise, we need to resist worldly thinking and show the world the beauty of the kingdom of God as revealed in Jesus. We definitely need to resist injustice wherever it is found, but in Jesus' name and according to God's Word. Yes, we need to repent where there has been racism, homophobia and abuse of leadership. We also need to hold firm to the truth and not be ashamed of the gospel. The Church needs us to get back to simple faith in God's Word and put it into practice. We need a fresh vision of the glory of God and the power of the gospel to cure our compromise.

In his insightful book *Disappearing Church* (2016), Mark Sayers writes:

> Post-Christianity is not pre-Christianity; rather post-Christianity attempts to move beyond Christianity, while simultaneously feasting upon its fruit. Post-Christian culture attempts to retain the solace of faith, whilst gutting it of the costs, commitments and restraints that the gospel places on the individual will. Post-Christianity intuitively yearns for the justice and shalom of the kingdom, whilst defending the reign of the individual will.[8]

He goes on to summarise that this is like wanting the kingdom without the King.[9] We must resist a version of justice without Jesus or Christianity without Christ.

Even non-Christian commentators such as Jordan Petersen and Douglas Murray have admitted that much of this new 'identity religion' has come about because of the loss of the Christian faith in the nation. John Mark Comer concludes that, 'The temptation to us

---

8   M. Sayers, *Disappearing Church: From cultural relevance to gospel resilience* (Chicago, IL: Moody, 2016), pp. 15–16.

9   Sayers, *Disappearing Church*, p. 80.

in the West is less to atheism and more to a DIY faith that's a mix of the Way of Jesus, consumerism, secular sexual ethics and radical individualism.'[10] We need to see compromise as the arid and futile distraction that it is and recover a compassionate, bold and love-filled radical discipleship that goes deeper than the surrounding culture. Our answer is always Jesus!

Enough!

At a recent New Wine United conference, Nicola Neal from Every Life was sharing about a remarkable outpouring of the Spirit in Uganda. She described the build-up to that outpouring as a time of holy desperation and found herself weeping and saying 'Enough!' to God. Enough of the compromise, enough of boring church, enough of not seeing God's power manifest! Do we have that thirst? Do we have that holy discontentment?

I want to echo Nicola's 'Enough!' over the Church living in compromise and self-sufficiency. Why are we so dehydrated as Church when we know Jesus, the source of living water?

We need to see what the Lord was showing Jeremiah. We need to pray, 'Bend me, break me, fill me, use me.' Jeremiah was a weeping prophet. The pain of his prophetic honesty would pierce the contemporary western Church. Maybe the modern prophetic ministry today needs to mature to become a weeping ministry.

I find it hard to write these chapters. I know some of us may be reading saying, 'Really? Can't we just enjoy church on Sundays? Can't we just love everybody and be nice and positive? You are being over the top. People are doing their best.' I do hear you, if that is your sentiment. No one wants to be the one pointing out the difficulties. I am sure we would all rather focus on the positives and just keep going.

---

10 J. M. Comer, *Live No Lies: Recognize and resist the three enemies that sabotage your peace* (London: Form, 2021), p. 228.

Can I say, I write as a lover of Jesus and his Church. I write as a pastor and leader. I write as one who shares in the struggles with you and I know my own deep failings. I love conversing with people and have a gentle heart for genuine discipleship struggles and circumstances of vulnerability and weakness. But, my heart also aches and cries out that all I am sharing is true. There is so much more. We are a compromising Church in the west. We are dry and unable to speak to our culture because we so often try to mimic it, rather than redeem it. I just long for more of God. There has got to be more than this. While we can acknowledge the complex reasons for our dryness, doesn't someone have to say 'Enough!' as long as it is said in love?

I used to reflect on this regularly while speaking at New Wine summer conferences. I would get up onto the platform to speak again on revival, and I would think to myself, 'Another year, and no revival yet.' I met many hungry people and we all seemed to be thinking the same thing, yet year after year, no breakthrough yet. Why not? Why is God not sending revival to the UK?

One of the reasons I find all this hard is because I see my own weakness. I see my own hardness, half-heartedness and shallowness and I ask a deeper question than why we don't have revival in the UK. I ask myself honestly: why is my own heart not as near to God as I want it to be? I need God! I need revival! What will it take to break my hard heart? I read the stories of revival with aching amazement, yet I am not willing to pay the price for such a revival in my own life. Are you?

Are we content to live like this and have the kind of Church we have for the years to come? We seem to have been so content up until now. We have the kind of lives and Church we really want, don't we?

No one likes an alarm. That piercing beeping is annoying, but important. I know that godly and hard-working leaders are doing the best they can and we still feel we are failing. My heart is for us

100 per cent. But, don't things need to change? Our hard work will not change our nation. Only the gospel can.

My heart is to free us from the tyranny of trying to bring revival by ourselves. We will be deeply disappointed because we are tired and dry without Jesus. Is it not time to be more straightforward about the lack of miracles, answered prayers and conversions to Christ? We have had a high expectation of church and a low expectation of God. Churches have to run very hard even to stand still. All the while our communities have been left unchanged by a half-gospel of being led to the cross, but not taking it up. Churches are full of active, caring, good people, but not yet saturated with power from the Spirit. We are often senti-mental about God, but not yet saturated with God. We need to humble ourselves.

There has been much excitement for revival and yet so little experience of it. God has not yet found someone through whom he wills to bring this next nation-changing move of the Spirit. I have noticed that some are trying to redefine revival. It has become a buzzword of optimism. Hype around revival will not help us to see it. The more we hype it up, the less likely we are to experience it. Unless we change, we might not see revival. It won't come by our assuming it will. Roy Hession said, 'Revival is not the roof blowing off, but the bottom falling out.'[11] What was meant by this? Having such a vision of God that we cry out that we are 'undone', as Isaiah did. Experiencing heartbrokenness for our sin. Dying in order to really live.

The path to power is not in adding a bit of creativity, experi-menting or tweaking. Growth does not come from initiatives, projects or courses. It is an ancient path. Having begun this chapter with Jeremiah, I have also been reflecting on his words in Jeremiah 6.16:

---

11 Roy Hession, *My Calvary Road* (Fearn: Christian Focus Publications, 1996), p. 14.

'Stand at the crossroads and look;
  ask for the ancient paths,
ask where the good way is, and walk in it,
  and you will find rest for your souls.
But you said, "We will not walk in it."'

Jeremiah is calling a people who have forsaken God (see Jer. 2.1–3, 11–14; 3.21–22). They were not rightly related to God. Something was missing. Something was out of place and fragmented. There were many other leaders in Jeremiah's time who were not telling the truth. They were prophesying 'peace, peace' (Jer. 6.14–15) but God had not sent them. They had no sensitivity to the dire need of the people. They were telling people, 'Don't worry, all is well. You're doing great.' Jeremiah was asking people to take 'ancient paths' back to God. These are the paths of the gospel, holiness, prayer, surrender and the anointing of the Spirit.

A number of years ago we had a prophetic word for our church:

Go after that which is deep and authentic. The ancient ways. They are not necessarily obvious . . . You need to ask for the way forward, the good way we need to go in. And walk in it, don't just know it, walk in it. Speak something ancient, authentic, real that challenges superficial modern consumerist spirituality.

We need to restore the ancient paths of prayer, the anointing of the Spirit, holiness of life, gospel power, caring for the poor and loving God and neighbour.

Broken cisterns mean a dry Church. We can't hold the water of the Spirit because we have chosen autonomy and unfaithfulness. This Church is unable to be filled. A broken cistern can't hold what it receives, so despite the parched world being ripe for revival, the dry Church can't hold the outpouring yet. Our souls are dry. We find ourselves in a desert, in great need of the water of the Spirit. But hope is not lost. Deserts are places of preparation. The Church is dry, but hope remains.

This ground is dry our hearts in need
God hear our cry your face we seek
Forgive us for the ways we've strayed from you
Un-stop the wells, cause springs to rise anew and

Pour out your Spirit, pour out your Spirit saturate us now
Saturate us now O God
Pour out your Spirit, pour out your Spirit saturate us now
Saturate us now O Lord our God

You send us to the nations now
Anoint us with your Spirit's power
Humbly we offer all to serve you Lord
O God revive us for your kingdom's cause and

Pour out your water on the land, pour out your water on the
land
Pour out your water on the land God.[12]

---

12 'This Ground is Dry', by Martin Huff, 2022.

3

'In the desert a highway':
heart preparation

> *A voice of one calling:*
> *'In the wilderness prepare*
> *the way for the LORD;*
> *make straight in the desert*
> *a highway for our God.'*
> (Isaiah 40.3)

Given the serious situation we find ourselves in, isn't it time we did something about it? It is time to pray for change and to live differently. Deserts in the Bible are robust places of spiritual formation and preparation (Isa. 40.3). Now is the time to prepare the way for the Lord in the UK.

God loves to move in deserts. He prepares and builds his highway so he can come and move. If we realise the truth that this is a dry time in the Church, we can receive God's call to prepare! We can hear his heart to make a much-needed highway for him to move in our lives.

What can happen in the desert?

Jesus was thoroughly prepared for his ministry. He lived for 30 years in hiddenness and unseen preparation and then went into the desert for 40 days of waiting, prayer, fasting and testing, just before it all kicked off. Jesus didn't cut corners and didn't move in spiritual power by accident. Jesus believed in wholehearted preparation.

Matthew 4 reminds us that Jesus was 'led by the Spirit into the wilderness' (verse 1) and returned in the power of the Spirit.

Jesus' remarkable ministry was not instant; it unfolded in the crucible of deliberate spiritual preparation, formation and building a highway of prayer, intimacy, dependency and love. Some of us want just a few minutes of prayer to be the gateway to a fruitful ministry. We spend a few brief moments in God's presence then expect to change the world. It didn't work like that for Jesus, so who do we think we are!

We are not great at preparing God's way. We prefer being active and busy doing things now, rather than making a highway for God in a tough desert environment. We find deserts disconcerting and want to get out of them as quickly as possible. We rarely ask: God, what are you doing in this desert? How do we want to shape and form our hearts in the desert?

We could do our deserts differently and invite God to fully prepare us. We could prepare the way for God to move in our lives. Preparation is slow. Have you noticed that God is not in a hurry, even though we often are? When God works, he is thorough. When God prepares us, it is not shallow. God wants us to seek his presence more than programmes. He wants us to trust him more than relying on general principles we have picked up third hand. He wants us to die to sin and take up our cross. All this work in us is his preparation and it takes time.

During the pandemic, I felt Isaiah 40.3 was a defining and compelling Scripture for the Church. In such a brutal time of wilderness, we were called to prepare the way for the Lord. The desert is designed to throw us back on God in repentance and prayer.

God was speaking about repentance and preparation during the pandemic. Were we listening? If ever there was a time to pray and repent of our sin and come back to God, that was it. But, did we? Have we continued on that highway for God in our lives? My prayer is that having been tested and stripped back, we are hungrier than ever for God to move. Not going back to how things were before, but seeking something more. I think we know we want to see a renewed Church emerge from all of this; so, 'Come, Holy Spirit'. The desert is tough, but also the perfect place for God to move in power.

The Holy Spirit is breaking, shaping and remoulding us for more fruitful mission and discipleship. He is preparing us in the desert. This is a beautiful but often painful preparation. We need more of the Holy Spirit to play our part in multiplying, equipping and sending disciples and ultimately revival! There are many challenges facing us all and sometimes we feel as though we have 'little strength' (Rev. 3.8). Life has become more uncomfortable and we don't know what is to come. Yet, it is also a moment of potential for revival. If only we would allow God to prepare us more.

Jesus started in the desert. This was the unattractive launchpad for the most incredible three years the world had ever seen. Jesus, the Living Water, had to start in the desert. What do we need to face so God will form us in a new way? What might be holding us back and hindering revival? What unattractive launchpad for revival might God bring into your life? Are you willing to embrace it?

God called Ezekiel into a valley of dry bones. He formed Moses and Paul in the desert, in a place of fasting, waiting, testing, obedience, surrender and prayer. There are so many men and women in history who went to God's school of the desert and found revival being birthed through them. People such as John Wesley, Amy Carmichael, Mary Slessor, William Booth and Duncan Campbell. God was at work, preparing hearts for revival.

Heart preparation for revival

We need to get ready for revival. The only way we can prepare is to prepare our hearts. During my teenage years, I used to listen every night to Duncan Campbell's sermon, *Heart Preparation for Revival*. His emphasis was on preparing by 'waiting upon God in prayer' and seeking a pure and 'clean heart'. As Campbell had experienced revival, and I had not, I thought it wise to listen to what he had to say. I always found it interesting that we could actually prepare for revival. What a thought! My heart preparation, or lack of it, could have a bearing on whether revival came.

Have you ever considered that your spiritual condition isn't just about you? If we prepare our hearts to get right with God and pray, God can move, and that can touch so many others. This is the message of 2 Chronicles 7.14 that:

> if my people, who are called by my name, will humble
> themselves and pray and seek my face and turn from their
> wicked ways, then I will hear from heaven, and I will forgive
> their sin and will heal their land.

The key word in that verse is the first word, 'if'. We can choose whether to prepare our hearts or not. We can choose whether to repent and pray or not. Our heart preparation or lack of it has huge and perhaps even eternal consequences not only for us, but for those around us.

So, how seriously are we taking our own preparation for revival? Are we doing anything to prepare our hearts? Are we allowing God to strip back our pride and self-reliance? Are we keeping our hearts clean before God? Are we getting to know God in prayer and seeking him for revival?

In April 2020 I became deeply aware of my own need for revival. My journal reflected the heart preparation going on. My prayer life needed to go deeper than simply crying out for God's mercy regularly. I wanted to know God more. Here are some brief journal reflections from when I was seeking God to do some heart preparation:

- 'I don't want to be a blind guide, false teacher, Pharisee.'
- 'Must not allow fear of man to rob me of blessing.'

- 'This is a time of personal revival – don't waste it'
- 'I feel embarrassed by my prayer poverty.'
- 'Revival is missing in me'
- 'Need for genuine love for our community.'

I was asking God to search me and seeking to examine my heart motives and my weaknesses, so I could bring them into the light of God's grace. My journal also bore witness to my wrestling to keep a right heart. I wrote one day, 'What comfort am I relying on? TV, food, working hard . . . Masking insecurities.' It is important to reflect on areas where we need God's grace, healing, discipline and empowering to change and prepare for revival.

When we seek heart preparation for revival, we will come face to face with temptation and strongholds regarding money, sex, fear, power, anger, pride, gluttony, self-sufficiency, unforgiveness, busyness, addiction . . . and much more. Proverbs 4.23 says to 'guard your heart, for it is the wellspring of life'.[1] We need to do the discipleship work of heart preparation so God can move in us and through us more and more.

This is hard and vulnerable work. It is uncomfortable and never-ending, yet so significant. I have found it helpful to use a journal and write out prayer topics for heart preparation for revival, so I can keep going and persevere in these areas. In my prayer journal, I wrote down John Mark Comer's 'hurry-sickness checklist' to keep myself alert to areas that I need to watch out for. These included irritability, hypersensitivity, relentlessness, workaholism, slippage of spiritual disciplines, emotional numbness, lack of care for your body, escapism, out of order priorities and isolation.[2] All these are areas where any of us might need God's mercy, grace and help. Dealing with

---

1   This wording is as in the 1978 and 1984 editions of the NIV; the 2011 edition gives, 'guard your heart, for everything you do flows from it.'

2   J. M. Comer, *The Ruthless Elimination of Hurry* (London: Hodder & Stoughton, 2019), pp. 48–51.

these shadows of the soul is part of heart preparation for revival. We need to get all our inner life issues into the light and under the power of the Holy Spirit. I had noticed a lack of spiritual power and mourned over it. But, I also knew that heart preparation and making a highway for God in my life was key to getting back on track. God has always been in the business of preparing hearts for his presence and power.

Let's take a look at some characters from Scripture being prepared for God to move in power. In Exodus 20.18–21 we see the awesome scene of God's raw power, which made the Israelites afraid. We read:

> When the people saw the thunder and lightning and heard
> the trumpet and saw the mountain in smoke, they trembled
> with fear. They stayed at a distance and said to Moses, 'Speak
> to us yourself and we will listen. But do not have God speak
> to us or we will die.' Moses said to the people, 'Do not be
> afraid. God has come to test you, so that the fear of God will
> be with you to keep you from sinning.' The people remained
> at a distance, while Moses approached the thick darkness
> where God was.

The people were kept from sinning by seeing God's glory, so they feared the Lord. This is heart preparation for revival.

This is not a time to pretend. We often imagine ourselves in the right. We believe our hearts to be good soil. But, are we, really? God loves us unconditionally, but our actions don't always please him. The Pharisee in Luke 18 justified himself. This is not the heart Jesus is looking for. Better to take the posture of the publican who cried to God for mercy over his soul. This is heart preparation for revival.

In John 13.37–38 we get a painful insight into Peter's heart issues:

> Peter asked, 'Lord, why can't I follow you now? I will lay
> down my life for you.' Then Jesus answered, 'Will you really

lay down your life for me? Very truly I tell you, before the
cock crows, you will disown me three times!'

Jesus knew the state of Peter's divided heart. Eventually, after some
time, and the pain of the denial and then the restoration on the
beach in John 21, Jesus succeeded in preparing Peter's heart for
Pentecost, and the power of God seen in Acts. This is heart preparation for revival.

We see heart preparation all over Scripture with every Bible
character, as God draws them closer to him, to receive mercy and
get right through into his presence and power. This process is not
always easy. Remember Jonah's disobedience and depression, yet
revival also transformed Nineveh. Remember David's lustful and
murderous actions, yet when restored he became a man after God's
own heart. These stories of heart preparation are everywhere. God's
people have been used to the school of the desert, where they are
refined and become ready for God to work.

I think we know something is missing. We miss God's presence
and can hear him calling us back. This is the basis of all heart preparation for revival. The sense that I must have God's presence return,
no matter what it costs. Mark Sayers writes about this process in its
various stages which lead us from the desert of spiritual exhaustion
to God's presence and power:[3]

1 *Holy discontent:* a deep dissatisfaction with the low state of our
   faith, the Church and the culture.
2 *Preparation:* deep work of preparation as God fills our hearts
   with his presence.
3 *Contending:* moving from consumption and passivity to
   contending for God's presence to come in power.

---

3 M. Sayers, *Disappearing Church: From cultural relevance to gospel resilience* (Chicago,
IL: Moody, 2016), pp. 69–166.

4 *Holy patterns:* reordering our priorities to welcome God's presence.
5 *The remnant:* a small group of people being renewed coming together to seek God.
6 *Renewal:* God's presence comes with power.

This process of heart preparation and repentance leads to transformation. It is a call to die, then really live. This is not particularly deep teaching; it is just that it has often been left undone. I also love that Sayers includes others in our process of renewal. We need one another in this journey of renewal.

This is beautifully illustrated in the moving story of how Duncan Campbell met with God afresh before he was used in the Hebrides Revival of 1949. Duncan had been converted to Christ, then was baptised with the Spirit in 1918, recovering from a cavalry charge in the First World War. He prayed the famous prayer of Robert Murray McCheyne: 'God make me as holy as it is possible for a saved sinner to be.'[4] God met powerfully with him and after the war he experienced the power of the mid-Argyll revival in the early 1920s.

In his testimony, Duncan Campbell went on to describe how he was later ordained as a Minister in the United Free Church of Scotland. He told of how God had blessed his ministry over these years, and he was even invited to teach at the Keswick Convention, which was one of the largest conferences of that time.

However, Campbell knew that despite his outward success he was spiritually barren after 17 years of ordained ministry. He spoke of his 'years of backsliding . . . a barren spiritual wilderness'.[5] He describes how he decided that he would either have to meet with God anew or resign from the ministry. He went home, went to his

---

4 B. H. Edwards, *Revival: A people saturated with God* (Darlington: Evangelical Press, 1990), p. 61.

5 A. Woolsey, *Duncan Campbell: A biography* (London: Hodder & Stoughton, 1974), p. 97.

study, lay on his rug beside the fire and began to cry out to God for mercy and a fresh infilling of the Spirit.

Campbell's teenage daughter, Sheena, seeing her father's distress of soul, went to speak with him and reminded him of how he had seen the mid-Argyll revival. She asked him the piercing question: 'Why is God not using you in revival today, Daddy?' Then added, 'When did you last lead a soul to Christ?'

This broke Duncan Campbell and he cried to God more than ever. It was said that at times those present in the house feared for his sanity, so great was his distress of soul and conviction of sin. The Spirit of God was doing a deep work of heart preparation for revival. Duncan Campbell's years of desert were about to end and the time of break-through came when God's mighty love swept over him. He writes:

> That night in desperation on the floor of my study, I cast myself afresh on the mercy of God. He heard my cry for pardon and cleansing, and as I lay prostrate before Him, wave after wave of Divine consciousness came over me, and the love of the Saviour flooded my being; and in that hour, I knew that my life and ministry could never be the same again.[6]

He received a fresh baptism of the Spirit and was transformed from that day on. From that experience was to come a man who led the Lewis Revival. Out of a desert and into revival, through the path of heart preparation.

The desert can be transformed

Are we, like Duncan Campbell, tired of living a dry, barren and unfruitful existence? God can lead us today through repentance and the baptism of the Holy Spirit into a new wave of revival.

---

6 D. Campbell, *God's Standard: Challenging sermons* (Edinburgh: The Faith Mission, 1964), p. 61.

Scripture holds out the wonderful promise that deserts can be transformed by the glory of the Lord:

> The desert and the parched land will be glad;
>   the wilderness will rejoice and blossom.
> Like the crocus, it will burst into bloom;
>   it will rejoice greatly and shout for joy.
> (Isaiah 35.1–2)

Isaiah 35 is like a refreshing glass of ice-cold water on a hot summer's day. Having said all we have about our parched world and dry Church, and the desert place of heart preparation, God now comes in power to cause the wilderness to blossom. The desert can come to life and be transformed and 'burst into bloom'.

On the other side of the pandemic, we have a gospel-moment to share Jesus, our living hope. I believe the more we let Jesus prepare us in the desert, the more we will see the desert bloom. I am passionate about seeing my local church of St Mary's thrive in times of revival! Despite the challenges over recent years, I have seen many people serving, putting others first, praying through trials, caring for others and leading them to Jesus. Alongside various trials, we have also seen blessings, such as new people coming, God providing financially and also we have seen people come to faith in Christ. God has been at work in a beautiful way in our Sunday services. This is all the ground of heart preparation and I believe the desert will give way to rejoicing greatly and shouting for joy!

Disturb us, Lord

Recently, I saw these words written on the wall of the Faith Mission Bible College in Edinburgh. They are attributed to Sir Francis Drake, written in 1577 before circumnavigating the globe. May God stir a holy discontent in us for the deserts in our lives to be transformed and for God to enlarge our hearts as he did with others before us. May God disturb us in the best way possible. May the parched world have a saturated Church to show the way to Jesus, the living water.

Disturb us, Lord,
When we are too pleased with ourselves,
When our dreams have come true
    because we dreamed too little,
When we arrived safely
    because we sailed too close to the shore.

Disturb us, Lord,
When with the abundance of things we possess,
    We have lost our thirst for the waters of life.
Having fallen in love with life,
    We have ceased to dream of eternity.
And in our efforts to build a new earth,
    We have allowed a vision of the new heaven to dim.

Disturb us, Lord,
To dare more boldly,
To venture on wilder seas,
    Where storms will show Your mastery.
Where losing sight of land,
    We shall find the stars.

We ask You to push back the horizons of our hopes.
And to push us into the future with strength, courage, hope
    and love.
This we ask in the name of our Captain,
    Who is Jesus Christ.

Part 2

A PEOPLE SATURATED WITH GOD

What could revival look like?

Into the desert, dryness and darkness God comes, and everything changes!

Our God is God of the impossible!

Just when the situation seems at its worst, God moves. This is the story of Scripture and salvation history. In times of crisis God sent Moses, Jonah, Esther, Deborah, Paul and many others. They were all born 'for such a time as this'. I believe you and I were born for this moment we find ourselves in. We were born for revival!

God loves to move through ordinary people in the most extraordinary ways. In a time of deep darkness, God chose an ordinary young woman, and in her womb was conceived the Light of the World. Mary's perfectly reasonable question to Gabriel in Luke 1.34 was, 'How will this be?' This might mirror our feelings for our troubled times. How can things ever change? How can the nation be changed? Is expecting revival too far-fetched or simply too difficult?

Yet, the answer from Gabriel to her question started with the transformational words which changed everything: 'The Holy Spirit will come on you . . .' The abundant answer to our situation today is for the Holy Spirit to come upon us, our churches and our land. Mary's testimony in Luke 1.37 was that 'nothing is impossible with God'. She gave her 'yes' to God and by faith welcomed God's miraculous incarnation into reality. God has always moved in the impossible.

We need a miracle in our land, and our God is the God of miracles. There is always hope because God hasn't finished with us yet. He is still speaking, moving and working. He is the God of salvation, resurrection, new life and living hope. There is hope for our nation. Jesus is so glorious. He is the source and spring of living water.

Revival is by definition a miracle and God has not run out of miracles. If only we could comprehend his unlimited power to save and transform. As God's people, we need a renewed vision of the immense glory and eternal capacity of God the Father, Son and Holy Spirit. He is altogether lovely, absolutely able, abundantly sovereign and more than enough! More will be done in a single week of revival than in years of ordinary church. Can churches have such a vision? I believe we can and we must! This is what it means to me to see local churches changing nations. May God fill every angle and facet of our vision. We need to be submerged in his glory, so we can see and know him rightly.

We may wonder whether local churches can really transform regions. What we really believe is possible will be linked to our vision of the grace, heart and power of God. Our God is the God of Abraham, Isaac and Jacob. He is Elijah's God who answered by fire; the God who brought his people out of Egypt and showed signs and wonders to the nations. This is our God. He is the same as ever. We are not seeking to be saturated with programmes, strategies or personalities; we need to be fully saturated with Almighty God!

I believe local churches can change even nations, but only when they are saturated, not dehydrated. We need to be saturated with God himself. His Spirit must flood and drench our lives and churches. There is much talk of 'resource churches' today, but what we really need is 'revival churches'.

Sadly, revival has often been misunderstood as mere excitement, religious entertainment or special efforts in mission, or a series of great meetings with a guest speaker. It has sometimes been confused with a healing crusade or a series of evangelistic services. Many also think of revival when they see visible manifestations of the Spirit such as shaking, falling or other signs and wonders. These may be wonderful, but they are not revival.

Revival reaches beyond a church and touches the whole community. God moves in such power that he is leading the movement and many are thoroughly converted to Christ. It is a sovereign move of the Holy Spirit upon both church and community in which God comes down in power. There is an extraordinary spiritual awakening that changes the whole community. Isaiah prayed, 'Oh, that you would rend the heavens and come down, that the mountains would tremble before you!' (Isa. 64.1).

> Let it come, O Lord, we pray Thee,
> Let the show'r of blessing fall.
> We are waiting, we are waiting,
> Oh, revive the hearts of all.[1]

Exploring what revival looks like

In this second part, over the next three chapters, let's explore what a revival could actually be like. I believe revival looks like floods on dry ground, the baptism of the Spirit and Jesus at the centre as never before. We will look at each of these.

Revival transforms villages, communities, towns, cities and regions. Revival is the outpouring of the life of Jesus into our neighbourhoods. As Arthur Wallis writes, 'The outpouring of the Spirit is likened in Scripture to a deluge of rain on a dry and thirsty land.'[2] Revival will bring the overwhelming presence of God across whole regions and the transformation of society. God will be manifest everywhere.

I will never forget visiting people on the Isle of Lewis who had lived through the Hebrides Revival of 1949–53. I met around six people from the revival. We sat together and there was a beautiful sense of the presence of God on our conversation. One of them said something I won't forget. She said, 'It's like we've lived in two

---

1 J. L. Black, 'God Is Here, and That to Bless Us', in *Songs of Victory* (Edinburgh: The Faith Mission, 1998), hymn 653.

2 A. Wallis, *Rain from Heaven* (London: Hodder & Stoughton, 1979), p. 93.

worlds.' Revival has an atmosphere of awakening the presence of God and eternity. Revival feels totally different to what we experience in an average church service today. Duncan Campbell used to describe revival as 'a people saturated with God'. Many people on Lewis testified to the reality that God was everywhere. Duncan Campbell described it as 'an awareness of God laying hold on the community'.[3] Other eyewitnesses from Lewis agreed, such as Norman Campbell, who said, 'You could sense and feel the presence of God everywhere. It was the power of God let loose. People were on their knees anywhere.' Annie Mackinnon added, 'I felt as if the Spirit of the Lord was in the very air one was breathing and it was just wonderful! The atmosphere was not just in church, but everywhere.' John Murdo Smith said:

A sense of the Lord's presence was everywhere . . . on the streets, in the shops, in the school – wherever people gathered revival was the topic of conversation. An unsaved man in Arnol said, when invited to the meetings, 'I don't need to go to the meetings to know that there is something supernatural going on in the village. I can feel it in my own home.'[4]

Let me share some of Duncan Campbell's eyewitness account of what revival on Lewis was like. It is important for us to get a sense of what revival feels like, looks like and could be like again in our time. Drink in this amazing account given when Duncan Campbell was preaching about the revival:

I preached in the church to a congregation of about 300, and I would say it was a good meeting, a wonderful sense of God. But, nothing really happened. I gave the blessing, and I am

3 D. Campbell, *God's Answer: Revival sermons* (Belfast: The Faith Mission, 1960), p. 72.
4 Various quotations from C. Peckham and M. Peckham, *Sounds from Heaven* (Fearn: Christian Focus Publications, 2004), pp. 90–1.

walking down the aisle when this young Elder came to me and said, 'Nothing has broken out tonight, but God is hovering over us and he will break through any moment.' Well I must be perfectly honest, I didn't feel anything. But here was a man much nearer to God than I was.

We are moving down the aisle and the congregation is moving out. They are all out now except this man and myself. He lifted his hands and started to pray, 'God, you made a promise to pour water on the thirsty and floods upon the dry ground, and God, you are not doing it.' He prayed and prayed and prayed again, until he fell on the floor in a trance. He is lying there and I am standing beside him for a few minutes.

And then the door of the church opened and another Elder came in. 'Mr Campbell, something wonderful has happened. Will you come to the door and see the crowd that is here?' 11 p.m. mind you. I went to the door and there must have been a congregation of between 600–700 people gathered around the church. This dear man stood at the door and suggested that we might sing a psalm, so he gave out Psalm 126, 'When Zion's bondage God turned back as men that dreamed were we, then was our mouth with laughter filled, our tongue with melody.' And they sang and they sang and they sang. And in the midst of it I could hear the cry of the penitent. I could hear men crying to God for mercy. I turned to the Elder and said, 'We had better open the doors again and let them in.'

And within a matter of minutes the church was crowded. Now where did the people come from? I cannot tell you. But I know that from village and hamlet the people came. They could only tell that they were moved by a power that they could not explain and the power was such as to give them to understand that they were hell-deserving sinners. And of course, the only place they could think of to find help was at the church.

There was a dance in progress that night in the parish and while this man was praying in the aisle the power of God moved into that dance and over 100 of the young people fled and made for the church. When I endeavoured to get up into the pulpit, I found the way blocked with young people who had been at the dance. I found a young woman lying on the floor of the pulpit crying, 'Is there mercy for me? Is there mercy for me? Is there mercy for me?' God was at work. That meeting continued until 4 a.m.

So, we left them there, and just as I was leaving the church, a young man came to me and said, 'Mr. Campbell, I would like you to go to the police station.' I said, 'The police station? What's wrong?' 'Oh,' he said, 'There's nothing wrong but there must be at least 400 people gathered around the police station just now.'

Now the sergeant there was a God-fearing man. I went along to that meeting. As I am walking along that country road – we had to walk about a mile – I heard someone praying by the roadside. I could hear this man crying to God for mercy. I went over and there were four young men on their knees at the roadside. Yes, they were at the dance but they are now there crying to God for mercy.

Now when I got to the police station, I saw something that will live with me as long as I live. The people are crying to God for mercy. Oh, the confessions that were made! There was one old man crying out, 'Oh, God, hell is too good for me! Hell is too good for me!' This is Holy Ghost conviction! Now mind you, that was on the very first night of a mighty demonstration that shook the island. Oh, let me say again, that wasn't the beginning of revival – revival began in a prayer meeting.

And, of course, after that we were at it night and day – churches crowded. A messenger would come – I remember one night it was after 3 o'clock in the morning – a messenger came to say that the churches were crowded in another parish 15 miles away. Crowded at that hour in the morning. We went, and I found myself preaching in a large church – a church that would seat 1,000 – and the Spirit of God was moving in a mighty way! I could see them falling, falling on their knees. I could hear them crying to God for mercy. I could hear those outside praying.

And that continued for, I'm sure, two hours. And then as we were leaving the church, someone came to me to tell me that a very large number of people had gathered on a field – they could not get into the church. They couldn't get into any of the churches. Along with the other ministers I decided to go. And here I saw this enormous crowd standing there as though gripped by a power that they could not explain. But the interesting thing about that meeting was a sight that I saw . . .[5]

This exceeding abundance seems beyond what we can ask for or imagine. It is hard to picture something we have never seen in our generation in the UK. We don't yet know what revival will mean in a social media-driven and digital world. It will impact every corner of culture and society, from art to music, from criminal justice to social reform. Education, media, business, government and the Church will all be impacted.

'Will you not revive us again?' (Ps. 85.6)

We are called to replant the gospel in our nation and prepare for revival. We have a responsibility for revival. God is sovereign, but we are also responsible.

Now is the time for floods. Now is the time for revival. Mark Sayers says, 'God chooses when and where and whom He will

---

5 Taken from a tape recording of Duncan Campbell, *The Lewis Revival*, Faith Mission Recordings.

renew. Yet we can prepare for His coming.[6] Who will accept their responsibility and prepare? Many Christians are sadly so taken up with their own 'little kingdoms' and personal satisfaction that there is little awareness of that responsibility and little time is given to preparation in repentance or prayer.

As I have reflected on my own journey and heart to prepare for revival, I think it is hard to quantify the impact of encounters with God's presence over the years, and the desire to see that, and much more, in the days to come.

I can remember meetings so full of God's presence on the Isle of Skye in the 1990s. My family went to a conference there each year run by The Faith Mission. There was a simple reverence and holiness, a no-frills approach, and the Word of God was preached in the power of the Spirit. After the main meetings, everyone poured into homes and hotels they were staying in for 'after meetings'. These meetings went on late into the night with heartfelt and spontaneous testimonies, prayers, hymn singing and a tangible sense of God's glory. This was not entertainment; it was real and also involved everyone. There was no hype or slick preacher. These were ordinary, spiritually thirsty people with a heart to seek God.

I also look back to student days in St Andrews University Christian Union. I served as Prayer Secretary and will never forget leading packed prayer meetings for revival, with people praying passionately, fervently and full of the Spirit. During those days, we went out onto the streets to share the gospel, we prayed fervently and we were united in a heart for revival. God blessed those times with a real sense of his nearness. These encounters shaped me and meant I could never settle for less than God's power manifest to the world. We need a demonstration of the Spirit's power. When we taste of the power of the Spirit, we are forever changed.

My journey has taught me that revival is possible. Our God is

6 M. Sayers, *Reappearing Church: The hope for renewal in the rise of our post-Christian culture* (Chicago, IL: Moody, 2019), p. 35.

able! I have immersed myself in reading about revival over the years, which also feeds that faith. Reading Scripture and church history and my own experiences remind me that our God is a covenant-keeping God. The lyrics of the modern worship song 'There is a Cloud' by Elevation Worship, with its evocative imagery of a holy cloud beginning to burst, bringing forth an end to spiritual dryness, is such a powerful image of revival. We know that faithfulness is God's very character. He never fails, disappoints or overpromises. I can see there is a cloud beginning to swell. My heart is for you to see it too.

4

'Floods on the dry ground': *communities transformed*

'But now listen, Jacob, my servant,
Israel, whom I have chosen.
This is what the LORD *says –*
he who made you, who formed you in the womb,
and who will help you:
Do not be afraid, Jacob, my servant,
Jeshurun, whom I have chosen.
For I will pour water on the thirsty land,
and streams on the dry ground;
I will pour out my Spirit on your offspring,
and my blessing on your descendants.
They will spring up like grass in a meadow,
like poplar trees by flowing streams.'
(Isaiah 44.1–4)

The simple answer to dryness is lots of water. God intends to bring floods of spiritual water into our lives. Floods of his presence, goodness, salvation and kingdom. Floods of healing, worship and love. Floods can cover whole regions and so it is with the life-giving floods of the Spirit. This is a beautiful picture of transforming lives across whole regions and nations.

A clear mark of revival in a community is that there is widespread gospel-transformation. It is like water reviving and refreshing dry ground. Just imagine streams of gospel life flowing out and bringing conviction, salvation, healing, restoration, reconciliation, wholeness, grace and power in your community. The presence and power of God flow out everywhere. That is why the best way to describe revival is as a saving, healing, life-giving and holy flood.

It is fantastic news in Isaiah 44 that God promises to 'pour water on the thirsty land'. Not just a trickle, but a flood, a stream of the Holy Spirit, is promised on their children. Wow! Isn't this absolutely what we need right now? If not for us, then for our children.

Such a flood of the Holy Spirit is our only hope as a nation. This picture of spiritual floods has often been associated with revival. It was this language from Isaiah 44 that inspired two elderly sisters of the Isle of Lewis who prayed over their community at a dry time when no young people were in the local churches. They prayed for the 'floods' and revival came.

There was something in these verses of Scripture that burned in the hearts of Christine and Peggy Smith, the two wonderful and elderly ladies from the Isle of Lewis who cried out to God for a new move of his Spirit in their day in 1949.[1] Their hearts were burdened by the lack of young people in churches across their community. They pleaded Isaiah 44.1–4 in prayer over months, day and night. Over and over they prayed and they would not take 'no' for an answer. They talked about 'giving ourselves to waiting upon God in prayer'. These two elderly women were near to God. They weren't alone either. There were praying people across the island of Lewis. People who remembered the revival of 1939 were once again crying out for a fresh flood on dry ground.

What did they see that we have missed? They saw the answer to spiritual dryness around them as the floods of the Spirit. It was as simple as that.

Here is how Duncan Campbell described the beginning of the Lewis Revival and the scenes of that revival:

---

1 For the full story, see A. Woolsey, *Duncan Campbell: A biography* (London: Hodder & Stoughton, 1974), p. 114.

This is how it began: A number of men and women were made to feel conscious of the desperate need of their parish, all human effort had failed and left them baffled. They realised that their one resource was to fall back on God. Oh, how true it is that despair often is the womb from which real faith is born . . . So they entered into a solemn covenant that they would not rest or cease from prayer until God sent revival.

According to the report given to me by the minister of the parish, you found men waiting through the night in the confidence that God was about to manifest His power. You find two elderly sisters on their faces before the peat fire three nights a week pleading one promise, I say one promise; 'I will pour water on him that is thirsty and floods upon the dry ground.' A promise made as they declared by a covenant-keeping God who must ever be true to His covenant engagements.

So, they waited and the months passed and the months passed and nothing happened; until one morning a young man in the congregation read a portion of Psalm 24, 'Who shall ascend into the hill of the Lord, or who shall stand in His holy place? He that hath clean hands and a pure heart . . . He shall receive the blessing of the Lord.' Looking around to his praying companions and speaking in Gaelic, he said: 'Brethren, it seems to me just so much humbug to be praying as we are praying, and to be waiting as we are waiting here, if we ourselves are not rightly related to God.' And then he prayed, 'Are my hands clean, is my heart pure?' He got no further. At that moment there came to them a realisation of God, an awareness of His presence that lifted them from the sphere of the ordinary into the sphere of the supernatural. Three of them fell prostrate on the floor. Revival had come and the power was let loose in that barn that shook the whole community of Lewis.[2]

---

2   D. Campbell, *The Price and Power of Revival* (London: Scripture Illustrations, 1956), pp. 59–62.

Again, Duncan Campbell describes revival breaking out in another community on Lewis:

> So, we met, there was about 30 of us and prayer began. I found it a very hard meeting. I found myself battling and getting nowhere as the hours passed. After midnight I turned to a young man in the meeting and said, 'John, I feel the time has come for you to pray.' That dear man rose to his feet and prayed and in his prayer he uttered words such as I had never heard in a prayer before. He said, 'O God you made a promise, are you going to fulfil it? We believe you are a Covenant-Keeping God, will you be true to your covenant? You have said you will pour water on the thirsty and floods upon the dry ground. I do not know how others stand in your Presence, but if I know my own heart, I know where I stand, and I tell Thee now that I am thirsty, oh thirsty for a manifestation of the man of Thy right hand. Lord, before I sit down I want to tell you that your honour is at stake.' Have you ever prayed like that? Here is a man praying the prayer of faith. Believe it or disbelieve it – verify this if you like – the house shook like a leaf, the dishes rattled on the sideboard. An elder said to me, 'Mr Campbell, an earth tremor', 'Yes' I said and closed the meeting, walking out to find the whole community ablaze with God.[3]

Are we not tired of trying to change things in our own strength? We can't change societies through initiatives or projects. Only God can save our nation. Commentators are crying out for real change in our world. It won't come from ideology, culture or fashions. It will come from the manifest presence of God. Real change comes from a sovereign flood of God in our towns, cities, rural communities, inner cities, suburbs and even across the nations.

---

3   Campbell, *Price and Power of Revival*, p. 66.

We need a flood-time of the Spirit

I don't think we have yet got to the place where we really believe this. Church still feels as if we think *we* can change things. I wonder how long it will take us to see that it is *God* we need. How we need him right now. How we need a nation-shaking, community-transforming, neighbourhood-saturating move of God. All things are possible as we call upon the God of Moses, David, Elijah and Daniel. We are living through a remarkable period in history. Could this be the time for a significant breakthrough?

Our God is the same as he ever was. He is still the only Saviour. He is our only hope. Listen to Isaiah's heart as others have done before us and prayed through for revival. What could he see when he wrote these words? What can't we yet see?

May we see that this is God's work of grace in us. Isaiah says in verse 3, '*I* will pour water.' Any revival must begin with God's outpouring upon us of his Spirit. In his meditations on these verses of Scripture, Robert Murray McCheyne wrote of how God begins this work with thirsty souls.[4] He wrote of our 'poor dry ground souls'. He said, 'You are the dry ground. What will God pour out on you? . . . Floods of grace, floods of the Spirit, floods of blessing.' McCheyne saw revival in Dundee and wrote of 'learning good hope of revival in our day'. His advice was, 'Learn, Christians, to pray for floods.'

McCheyne also wrote:

There is nothing more distressing in our day than the want of growth among the people of God. They do not seem to press forward . . . When I compare this year with last year, what is the difference? How different things are when the Spirit is poured out! The children of God will be like willows. You have

---

4   *Sermons of Robert Murray McCheyne* (Edinburgh: Banner of Truth, 2000), pp. 14–18.

seen the willow, how it is always growing, day or night, ever growing, ever shooting out new branches. If you cut it down, it springs up again. So would you dear Christian, if there was a flood-time of the Holy Spirit. Then there would be less care about your business, more love of prayer and sweet praises.[5]

I began to desire the floods of the Spirit while still a teenager in Scotland. I went to a good church, but was not burdened for much more until I began to hear about the revivals past in Scotland. I listened to the preaching of Duncan Campbell every night for years, sometimes two sermons each night. I became thirsty to see something in my day and time. I saw how dry the Church was compared to what I heard about former times.

I read as much as I could about revivals. I bought Colin Whittaker's classic book, *Great Revivals* (1984). When I discovered stories of how whole communities and nations had been changed by the Holy Spirit fully possessing the church and thousands upon thousands being converted to Christ, I could never be the same again. I was coming to the conviction that God was not finished yet. There would be outpourings to come and I wanted to be part of that. Reading revival history showed me how God had not only moved across the UK and America during times of great awakening during the eighteenth and nineteenth centuries, but also across Latin America, Africa and Asia. There have been outstanding moves of revival in nations such as Brazil, Armenia, Indonesia, India, China and Korea. It is well known that the fastest-growing church today is in Iran. Revival is worldwide and while the UK has seen great things over generations, there is such a glorious heritage of gospel life transforming communities all over the world.

I can't recommend highly enough reading the stories of people like Martin Luther, John Wesley, George Whitefield, Charles Finney,

---

5   R. M. McCheyne, *The Best of Robert Murray McCheyne: 120 daily devotions to nurture your spirit and refresh your soul* (Reno, NV: Honor Books, 2006), p. 158.

Evan Roberts, Charles Spurgeon, Robert Murray McCheyne, David Brainerd, Amy Carmichael, Jonathan Goforth, John Hyde, D. L. Moody, William and Catherine Booth, John George Govan, Duncan Campbell and many more, including Bakht Singh from India, John Sung of China and Peterus Octavianus from Borneo. Floods of the Spirit have been poured out over the years across the nations. I firmly believe that we should all become students of revival history.[6]

Revival is totally different from evangelism because it results not only in full churches, but in transformed culture and society. There are numerous examples of when this has occurred in the UK in the past. The year 1859 was described as the 'Year of Grace' in the UK, as approximately one million people came to faith in Christ in that one year.[7] At least 10 per cent of the population of Northern Ireland were converted to Christ in one year.[8] Many of us have heard of the mighty Welsh revival of 1904 where 100,000 people were saved. Did you know that Indonesia saw a remarkable revival converting Muslims to Christ in the 1960s and 1970s? There is currently revival in China and a remarkable flood-time of the Spirit in Iran. History is filled with revivals, and in many parts of the world, it continues to this day.

Evan Roberts led the Welsh revival in 1904. Here is what he said about a meeting during the first week of that remarkable move of God:

> By midnight the whole congregation was overwhelmed with tears . . . Then the people came down from the gallery and sat close to one another. 'Now', said I, 'we must believe the Spirit

---

6 I would strongly recommend starting with *Sounds from Heaven* by Colin and Mary Peckham (Fearn: Christian Focus Publications, 2004). It is an amazing series of eyewitness accounts of the revival on the Isle of Lewis.

7 C. Whittaker, *Great Revivals* (Basingstoke: Marshalls, 1984), p. 82.

8 W. Duewel, *Revival Fire* (Grand Rapids, MI: Zondervan, 1995), p. 171.

will come; not think He will come; not hope He will come; but firmly believe that He will come'. Then I read the promises of God and pointed out how definite they were. After this the Spirit said that everyone was to pray . . . pray and believe and wait. And this is the prayer, 'Send the Spirit now, for Jesus Christ's sake.' The prayer began with me. Then it went from seat to seat – boys and girls, young men and maidens. Some asking in silence, some aloud, some coldly, some with warmth, some formally, some in tears . . . I felt the place beginning to be filled, and before the prayer had gone half way through the chapel, I could hear some brother weeping and sobbing and saying, 'Oh dear! dear! well! well!' On went the prayer, the feeling becoming more intense, the place being filled more and more . . . Some called out, 'No more Lord Jesus, or I die'. Others cried for mercy, weeping, singing and lying prostrate on the floor in agony of conviction for their sin. Eventually they closed the meeting and Evan Roberts got to bed at 3:15am.[9]

In his great book, *Revival Fire* (1995), Wesley Duewel goes on to write of Evan Roberts:

Roberts began to pray for 100,000 souls and God gave him the assurance that 100,000 would be won to Christ. He testified, 'The divine fire has taken hold of us.' Roberts felt the necessity of full obedience to the leading of the Holy Spirit. He envisaged taking a team of young people with him to evangelise across Wales. He kept urging the people to surrender fully to the Holy Spirit and to obey Him. God came upon Evan mightily as he prayed. One night he could not sleep. 'The room was so full of the Holy Spirit. The outpouring was so overwhelming

---

9 Duewel, *Revival Fire*, pp. 189–90.

that I had . . . to plead with God to stay His hand.' God gave His servant visions in those days during prayer times. In one vision Roberts saw the vast fiery pit of hell surrounded by a wall with one door. He saw a surging mass of people as far as the eye could see coming toward the pit. He pled with God to shut hell's door for one year. In another vision Roberts saw a brilliant moon and an arm stretched out to the world. He saw the vision again and this time the hand held a piece of paper on which was written, '100,000'.[10]

I love this heart of Evan Roberts for the floods of the Spirit over Wales. I often think about my own community here in Epping Forest, Essex, which has over 130,000 people. How we need the floods of the Spirit here to sweep them into God's kingdom. Colin Whittaker writes of the Welsh revival:

The presence of the Lord was felt everywhere . . . The whole of Wales was now affected. Hardened unbelievers were gloriously converted. Drunkards, thieves and gamblers were transformed. Confessions of awful sins were heard on every side. Old debts were paid . . . Courts had few cases to try. Dance halls were deserted and pubs were empty, but prayer meetings were crowded.[11]

This is what I think we need to see as revival. God at work! Here is another example of revival in Wales, but this time from 1743, as Howell Harris speaks about Daniel Rowland:

O such power as generally attends the labours of brother Rowland, it is indeed uncommon and almost incredible until

---

10 Duewel, *Revival Fire*, pp. 186–7.
11 Whittaker, *Great Revivals*, pp. 94–6.

one sees it himself. Their singing and praying is full of God! O how did my soul burn with sacred love as I was among them. They fell almost as dead by the power of the Word, and continue weeping for joy having found Jesus. Some mourn under a sense of their vileness and some in the pangs of new birth.[12]

We need streams in the desert

Isaiah 35 speaks of the similar picture of streams in the desert as a place of transformation, refreshing and renewal (see also Ps. 1.3; Hos. 6.2). I love how verse 6 describes water gushing forth in the wilderness. What a powerful image and also something that seems impossible. Notice the contrast from burning sand to a pool and thirsty ground to bubbling springs. I love these revival images:

Water will gush forth in the wilderness
     and streams in the desert.
The burning sand will become a pool,
     the thirsty ground bubbling springs.
(Isaiah 35.6–7)

Streams are linked to healing, miracles, the impossible becoming possible, incredible joy, praise and worship, exuberance, passion, dynamism and transformation. The water 'gushes'. This is what God does. He comes and suddenly everything changes. I love the 'suddenly' of God. This was what happened at Pentecost. 'Suddenly' there was a gush of the Holy Spirit. An outpouring, bursting forth, a saturation and soaking. God comes and things change.

Remember reflecting on the dry world and dehydrated Church? These verses in Isaiah paint a new picture of saturating-hope

---

12 B. H. Edwards, *Revival: A people saturated with God* (Darlington: Evangelical Press, 1990), p. 11.

when God is on the move. Isaiah rejoiced to see dry ground flooded. Are we thirsty as they were, or are we just too busy or otherwise occupied? I believe we need a real vision of streams in the desert in our time. God is more than able to supply the floods we need.

The psalmist also saw this picture of streams of water. He writes:

Blessed is the one
   who does not walk in step with the wicked
or stand in the way that sinners take
   or sit in the company of mockers,
but whose delight is in the law of the LORD,
   and who meditates on his law day and night.
That person is like a tree planted by streams of water,
   which yields its fruit in season
and whose leaf does not wither –
   whatever they do prospers.
(Psalm 1.1–3)

More streams! We need streams to flow today. Streams in our cities, our schools and streets. Streams of living water. We are called to be planted by such streams. We are to be planted in the blessing of God. Life and fruitfulness flowing into our communities. This is revival.

God comes like spring rain

The harvest is dependent on the rain. We need rain in the wilderness if we are to get floods and streams of life. Drought was a clear sign of judgement in the Old Testament (Deut. 11.17; 2 Chron. 6.26) and having rain fall was a sign of divine favour (Deut. 28.12; 1 Kings 8.36). Just before the famous verse on revival in 2 Chronicles 7.14, we read that God is able to 'shut up the heavens so there is no

rain . . .' (verse 13) as a sign of his displeasure. Yet, he also then says
in verse 14 following on:

> if my people, who are called by my name, will humble
> themselves and pray and seek my face and turn from their
> wicked ways, then I will hear from heaven, and I will forgive
> their sin and will heal their land.

Floods, streams and rain are a sign, particularly in the Old
Testament, of God's restoration, renewal and revival. The people
of God were well aware of their need for rain. Isaiah 55.10 says,
'As the rain and the snow come down from heaven, and do not
return to it without watering the earth and making it bud and
flourish, so that it yields seed for the sower and bread for the
eater . . .' Job 29.23 says, 'They waited for me as for showers and
drank in my words as the spring rain.' Jeremiah 14.22 gives this
reminder: 'Do any of the worthless idols of the nations bring
rain? Do the skies themselves send down showers? No, it is you,
LORD our God. Therefore our hope is in you, for you are the one
who does all this.'

Perhaps one of the most well-known Bible passages on rain is
Hosea 6.1–3:

> 'Come, let us return to the LORD.
> He has torn us to pieces
>   but he will heal us;
> he has injured us
>   but he will bind up our wounds.
> After two days he will revive us;
>   on the third day he will restore us,
>   that we may live in his presence.
> Let us acknowledge the LORD;
>   let us press on to acknowledge him.

As surely as the sun rises,
    he will appear;
he will come to us like the winter rains,
    like the spring rains that water the earth.'
(Hosea 6.1–3)

While it is obvious that literal rains are good for the earth, there is also a deeper spiritual picture here. Hosea is calling Israel to repentance. This heart to return to the Lord is key to revival. The desire to get right with God is the starting point towards healing and restoration. Such renewal always involves a breaking and healing. Real conviction of sin breaks us and also heals us. Having a broken heart over sin is part of returning to the Lord, coming out of spiritual dryness and preparing for the rain of God to come to revive us.

The beauty of this passage is in its gentleness. There is an intimacy in the restoration of a sinful people who go through brokenness over sin and then a binding of wounds, a healing, a restoration so that we may 'live in his presence'. God's purpose is for his people to know and encounter him as healer and restorer.

If we want to encounter God, we must 'press on' to seek him, to 'acknowledge' him. As we seek the Lord earnestly and press in to his presence, he will come to us. This is revival. The phrases in verse 3, 'he will appear' and 'he will come to us', are the essence of encountering God in renewal. How we need God to come. Revival history is filled with such encounters as God comes and reveals himself to people.

One such encounter was experienced by John Girardeau, in a move of the Spirit in North Carolina in 1858:

He received a sensation as if a bolt of electricity had struck his head and diffused itself through his whole body. Then he said, 'The Holy Spirit has come . . .' Immediately he began exhorting them to accept the Gospel. They began to sob softly like the falling of rain, then with deeper emotion to weep bitterly or to rejoice loudly . . . The meeting went on day and night for eight weeks.[13]

This encounter was marked by a sense that God had come like rain. Can we see how not only are we pursuing God, but first and foremost, God is pursuing us? God is eager to come to us. This is grace, this is the gospel and this is revival. God comes to us, and he comes to us like rain. This is gentle, so intimate and so refreshing.

The image of rain is not accidental. The early winter rain softened the ground and the later spring rains brought the growth. God wanted the rain to teach his people that having depended on the rain physically, there was also to be a spiritual dependence on God. Rain for their souls, rain for their revival. Rain brings softening, growth and new life. God is speaking through rain about his heart to revive his people. The words of Hosea were fulfilled when the Spirit came at Pentecost. God brought 'times of refreshing' (Acts 3.19) from his presence.

The floods, streams and rain of the Spirit are all about transforming communities by the gospel of the kingdom. When the water of the Spirit saturates lives, everything changes. The prayer to 'pour water on the thirsty and floods on the dry ground' is one of the greatest prayers we can pray for revival in our own time. May God submerge us, saturate us, flood our lives, stream into our souls and rain on us with his Spirit. This is revival!

Ho, ev'ry one that is thirsty in spirit
Ho, ev'ry one that is weary and sad;
Come to the fountain, there's fulness in Jesus,
All that you're longing for, come and be glad.

---

13 Edwards, *Revival*, pp. 11–12.

I will pour water on him that is thirsty,
I will pour floods upon the dry ground;
Open your heart for the gift I am bringing;
While you are seeking Me, I will be found.

Child of the world, are you tired of your bondage?
Weary of earth-joys, so false, so untrue?
Thirsting for God and His fulness of blessing?
List to the promise, a message for you![14]

---

14 L. J. Rider, 'Ho! Everyone That Is Thirsty in Spirit', in *Songs of Victory* (Edinburgh: The Faith Mission, 1998), hymn 565.

5

'Come to me and drink':
Jesus at the centre

On the last and greatest day of the festival, Jesus stood and said in a loud voice, 'Let anyone who is thirsty come to me and drink. Whoever believes in me, as Scripture has said, rivers of living water will flow from within them.' By this he meant the Spirit, whom those who believed in him were later to receive. Up to that time the Spirit had not been given, since Jesus had not yet been glorified.
(John 7.37–39)

Jesus is the source of living water. It is all about Jesus!

Let me say again, revival really is all about Jesus and always about Jesus!

Revival is rediscovering that Jesus is all in all. Jesus is the heart of revival. We need the Church to come back to putting Jesus at the centre. Jesus is the source of revival. The giver of the Holy Spirit. God moves most when we repent and return to Jesus, who gives the Spirit without measure. Before we 'go' we need to 'come and drink'. The people of God need the power of the Spirit more than ever. Revival is 'a new discovery of Jesus'.[1]

In a recent post on Facebook, Mike Pilavachi wrote:

Keep talking about revival and you are likely to end up with disappointed and disillusioned people; keep talking about

---

1 D. Campbell, *God's Standard: Challenging sermons* (Edinburgh: The Faith Mission, 1964), p. 61.

Jesus and you are likely to end up with revival. Our greatest need in the church is for more knowledge and experience of Jesus. Not more hype or a better show. Just Jesus.[2]

In February 1904, revival power saturated a meeting in New Quay in South Wales, as Florrie Evans, a timid 16-year-old girl, wept aloud, stood up and said, 'Oh I love Jesus Christ with all my heart.'[3] Isn't this the absolute heart of what we need today; a fresh baptism of extravagant love for Jesus? The Church is the bride of Christ and at her best when fully in love with her matchless bridegroom. We need to come to Christ, grow in Christ and drink of Christ Jesus. May our affection, passion and devotion be for our first love: Jesus.

It is deeply refreshing and sadly rare to meet Christians who overflow with simple, humble and active love for Jesus. They live from the secret place of adoration, intimacy, sacrifice, grace and worship. There is a sense of the love of Jesus being a love like no other.

I love the simplicity in Jesus' words in John 7 about being thirsty and coming to him to drink. So clear; such an invitation and wide-open offer. Anyone thirsty for God? Anyone seeking truth? 'Come to me and drink.'

Thirsty for more of Jesus

Meditating on this Scripture, Robert Murray McCheyne preached, 'Drink deeply of Christ's goodness . . . O how many people seem to come to Jesus and don't drink.'[4] Are we such people? Have we come to Jesus, but neglected to keep drinking from his living water? Do we drink deeply or just take a little sip? Our nation needs

---

2 Mike Pilavachi has given his permission to use his Facebook quote.

3 W. Duewel, *Revival Fire* (Grand Rapids, MI: Zondervan, 1995), p. 182.

4 R. M. McCheyne, *The Best of Robert Murray McCheyne: 120 daily devotions to nurture your spirit and refresh your soul* (Reno, NV: Honor Books, 2006), p. 144.

deep drinkers of Jesus; Spirit-filled, gospel-soaked, prayer-saturated people who live out John 7.37 as a testimony.

Encounter is so much more important than activity. Many of us are busy doing things for God, but without God's power. We are hard-working, but spiritually impotent. Perhaps we have treated coming to Jesus as a concept or theory, rather than an actual and real relationship. We are working for Jesus, but not drinking from Jesus, or overflowing with Jesus.

I think we do want to be saturated with God, but are often just too preoccupied with living complex lives. There are multi-layered reasons why we are not where we want to be spiritually. Perhaps we have neglected discipline, so don't have holy habits of prayer? Perhaps we struggle to get time to set aside and it just never happens? Perhaps we are simply so tired with the pressures of modern life? Perhaps we are apprehensive of the implications of a fuller devotion? Or fearful of what a more radical Christian life might mean for the way we live? Do we have the energy to really go for it with God? Life is just so busy for so many people.

Are we satisfied to keep going on with what we have now? Is that why we don't come and drink? Do we care about the missing revival? Does it bother us? We seem to labour so hard for so little return. So much energy for such little fruit.

We are perhaps too able, organised and well resourced with our own strength. We need to come and drink. We need the Holy Spirit and the difference the Spirit makes in prayer, evangelism, mission and justice. Many of us are exhausted; we have worked hard, trying and trying again, but with no spiritual power. This is true in every sphere of life and we can feel so discouraged. How can we get back to where God wants us to be?

I know all these layers of frustrated Christian experience. These and many others! As I reflect on my journey, and on the western Church, don't we need to adequately diagnose our Jesus-dehydration so we can change? I am not seeking to condemn, not at all. But, I do pray for the conviction of the Spirit on us all, so we may run to Jesus and actually drink.

Drink deeply of Jesus

What then does it mean to 'come to me and drink'? Before we move to thinking about the 'drinking' part Jesus told us to do, let's just remember that he told us to come to *him*. Jesus said, 'Come to me.' Perhaps this is where we can uncover more of our need. Often, if we are honest we come to meetings, services, conferences, counsellors, pastors, leaders and events. We come to church and all its amazing trappings, but have we actually paused and considered that we need to come to Jesus? It is possible even to sing worship songs, pray prayers, get challenged by good teaching and still not come to Jesus himself.

We are followers of Jesus and have access to him by faith through grace. Charlotte Elliott in her hymn 'Just as I am' put these thoughts into words in a way that helps:

Just as I am, without one plea,
But that thy blood was shed for me,
And that thou bidst me come to thee
O Lamb of God, I come.

Just as I am, and waiting not
To rid my soul of one dark blot,
To thee, whose blood can cleanse each spot,
O Lamb of God, I come.

Just as I am, though tossed about,
With many a conflict, many a doubt,
Fightings within and fears without,
O Lamb of God, I come.

Just as I am, thy love unknown
Has broken every barrier down,
Now to be thine, yea, thine alone,
O Lamb of God, I come.[5]

If we are to be rehydrated, filled and overflowing with the Spirit, we first need to come to Jesus and drink. This drinking is really about fully, regularly and deeply receiving from Jesus. We need more and more of him. We can come day by day and moment by moment to learn of him, lean on him, rest in him, listen to him, hear his voice, know his presence and be equipped with his power. This image of drinking means it is to be every day, constant and fresh. We need to drink throughout every single day. We are being invited to come to Jesus throughout every day. What a privilege and encouragement to be so close to Jesus.

Come to me and drink!

I believe if Jesus is at the centre of everything, revival will come. We don't pursue revival; we pursue Jesus. We drink from him and will overflow with him and never thirst again! Jesus is enough. He is sufficient to meet the needs of our nation. Jesus is the giver of the Spirit. Jesus is all we really need to see a move of God's Spirit in our day.

Our church vision is *Every Person, Every Place, Saturated with God*. That isn't something we can do or organise, budget for or plan. Only by fixing our eyes on Jesus can we see that vision come to pass. No church will be big enough for what God wants to do. God is calling you to take his gospel into every place: workplaces, schools, hospitals, homes; wherever he has sent you. Jesus can turn our communities the right way up.

---

5   C. Elliott, 'Just as I Am, Without One Plea', in *Songs of Victory* (Edinburgh: The Faith Mission, 1998), hymn 339.

We are relying so much on human endeavour, and not the Holy Spirit. Jesus told his disciples in Acts 1 to wait on his gift before doing anything. This nation is waiting for the Church to wait! Waiting is part of going! Wait until you have received power. Waiting is similar to drinking. It is receiving all God has for us so we can give it away.

> When we wait upon God, we drink.
> When we worship, we drink.
> When we pray, we drink.
> When we receive from Jesus, we drink.
> When we obey the Holy Spirit, we drink.
> When we serve the poor, we drink.
> When we share the gospel, we drink.
> When we take sabbath rest, we drink.

Anything we do in relationship and healthy connection with Jesus means we are drinking in his life and love. It is about being close to him and constantly dependent each day on him. What a beautiful way to live. Isn't it strange that we often default to neglecting this way of living and walking by faith?

We want much more of Jesus

In all our reflections on the missing revival, spiritual dryness, the need of the Church and the state of the world, my heart is for us to see how everything centres and rests on Jesus. The Lord Jesus is the living water we need. The further we get from Jesus, the more sin will lead us into dryness. The closer we get to Jesus, the more saturated we will be and the more we will be refreshed in his presence.

We need much more of Jesus. More of him in our lives, our homes, churches and communities. Sad to say, many homes and churches trundle on through life without any reference to Jesus. I believe the more of Jesus we see, the more likely revival will come.

At New Wine in 2022, Jon Tyson shared some teaching I heard on revival. He spoke of how he had learned in his study of revival that God comes where people want him. He called us to welcome Jesus in our lives, our homes, our churches and our communities. We want much more of Jesus. Lord Jesus, you are welcome in my life. You are welcome in my home and family. You are welcome in my church. You are welcome in my local area. You are welcome in the UK.

It is clear that Jesus is the giver of revival. He is the source of salvation. Revival really is Jesus moving in our lives in a transforming way. In *Set Me on Fire* (2015), I wrote about one man from the Lewis Revival telling me of his experience of the revival saying, 'It was as though Jesus had come to stay in the village.' May we get to know Jesus this way, so we see more of him moving around us. We need Jesus to come and stay with us.

Revival looks like Jesus

I believe Scripture uses water as a way of showing us and revealing who God is. It is a picture or image helping us grasp and see the truth of God's work in us. In the John 7 passage, Jesus taught that the Spirit was the living water that flowed when anyone came to him.

In Psalm 23.2 we read, 'He makes me lie down in green pastures, he leads me beside quiet waters . . .' This is his living water of life that also brings such refreshment and rest. In Psalm 23.5 we read that 'my cup overflows', speaking of the outworking of blessing. This is being filled to overflowing with the Holy Spirit. On this, Roy Hession quotes Andrew Murray saying, 'Just as water ever seeks and fills the lowest place, so the moment God finds you abased and empty, His glory and power flow in.' Hession goes on to say, 'The picture is that of the human heart as a cup which we hold out to Jesus, longing that He may fill it with the water of life.'[6]

In Ezekiel 43.1–2 we read:

> Then the man brought me to the gate facing east, and I saw the glory of the God of Israel coming from the east. His voice was like the roar of rushing waters, and the land was radiant with his glory.

This is echoed in Revelation 1.12–16:

> I turned round to see the voice that was speaking to me. And when I turned I saw seven golden lampstands, and among the lampstands was someone like a son of man, dressed in a robe reaching down to his feet and with a golden sash round his chest. The hair on his head was white like wool, as white as snow, and his eyes were like blazing fire. His feet were like bronze glowing in a furnace, and his voice was like the sound of rushing waters. In his right hand he held seven stars, and coming out of his mouth was a sharp, double-edged sword. His face was like the sun shining in all its brilliance.

Verse 15 describes the voice of Jesus as 'like the sound of rushing waters'. Can we see how the Scriptures regularly use the picture of water to draw us to the Lord and to reveal his glory? We need a flood of the voice of Jesus in our land. We need streams of justice and righteousness. We need the rain of revelation and healing. We need to be saturated with God himself and to know God himself. Revival is not for its own sake. It is to reveal Jesus to the Church and the world. I want revival to sweep into our land so that thousands

---

6   R. Hession, *The Calvary Road* (London: CLC, 1974), p. 16.

and millions of others will find the living water of salvation in Christ.

I love these verses in Revelation 7.14–17:

And he said, 'These are they who have come out of the great tribulation; they have washed their robes and made them white in the blood of the Lamb. Therefore,
'they are before the throne of God
    and serve him day and night in his temple;
and he who sits on the throne
    will shelter them with his presence.
"Never again will they hunger;
    never again will they thirst.
The sun will not beat down on them,"
    nor any scorching heat.
For the Lamb at the centre of the throne
    will be their shepherd;
"he will lead them to springs of living water."
    "And God will wipe away every tear from their eyes."'

Jesus is the centre. He is the Lamb on the throne and he is our Shepherd in Psalm 23. What an amazing promise that 'never again will they thirst'. The scorching heat will have no effect now because they are safe in Jesus for eternity. We will come back to this later, but our hope in Jesus means that he satisfies us with living water in this life and also in heaven, which is a city with a river running through it and an abundance of water.

The Shepherd 'will lead them to springs of living water and God will wipe away every tear from their eyes'. This is a verse that should bring every believer such strength and hope. Although we live in a dry and parched land, the day is coming when Jesus will return for his people and we will be led to springs of living water in heaven.

Now do we see more of the beauty, wonder and glory of Jesus? From his authority, lordship, leadership, love, power and goodness, he gives us living water in a dry, parched land. He refreshes us daily and one day will lead us into an abundant heavenly home. Staying close to Jesus should be our top priority.

At a recent New Wine Leadership conference, we welcomed the Spirit to come among us. Although there were over a thousand people in the conference, I heard the voice of the Lord whisper to me. He simply said, 'I love you.' And I just wept in his presence. I had come to that conference feeling exhausted, running on empty and thirsty for a fresh touch of Jesus. Let me tell you that such an encounter with Jesus makes all the difference. All it takes is one sentence from him and everything changes. His voice is the sound of many waters. We need a daily deep drink of Jesus to sustain, rehydrate and saturate our souls.

What does revival look like? It looks like Jesus. As A. R. Cousin puts it in 'The Sands of Time are Sinking':

O Christ! He is the fountain,
The deep, sweet well of love;
The streams on earth I've tasted
More deep I'll drink above:
There to an ocean fullness
His mercy doth expand,
And glory, glory dwelleth
In Immanuel's land.[7]

---

7   A. R. Cousin, 'The Sands of Time are Sinking', in *Songs of Victory* (Edinburgh: The Faith Mission, 1998), hymn 537.

6

'Baptise you with the Holy Spirit': *power from heaven*

John answered them all, 'I baptise you with water. But one who is more powerful than I will come, the straps of whose sandals I am not worthy to untie. He will baptise you with the Holy Spirit and fire.'
(Luke 3.16)

This sacramental experience of baptism is perhaps one of the most powerful truths in Scripture. It calls us to be soaked, immersed, drenched and saturated in God. This baptismal experience points to a reality of entire cleansing and miraculous empowering.

John's baptism with water was for repentance. Jesus' baptism, built on that foundation, was also a baptism of the Holy Spirit and fire. God longs for us to overflow with both repentance and power. God wants to flood, fill, saturate and steep you in his holy love, truth and power. This is his will for you. Your soul was not meant to be parched, but doused in God's glory. Baptism is where God reveals his eternal plan for us to be saturated with his glory.

If we want to understand what revival would be like, we need to meditate on the truth and experience of baptism, both in water and in the Spirit. Have you been baptised with water and also with the Holy Spirit? Speaking to Nicodemus in John 3.5, 'Jesus answered, "Very truly I tell you, no one can enter the kingdom of God unless they are born of water and the Spirit."' We need to be both saved and transformed so we become immersed in God.

Baptism is less a rite than a calling. It is meant to be a way of life, not just an event. In baptism we are marked as belonging wholly to Christ. We frequently think of baptism in an overly religious way, which hides its power and significance. It is perhaps the most beautiful picture of discipleship possible. It is a sign of a God-filled life. It is a sacrament of full surrender and a symbol of resurrection identity and new life.

Baptism is more all-encompassing, radical, deep-seated, profound, far-reaching and life-defining than we have perhaps realised. I think we treat it too lightly. We think we know what baptism means, but I believe we need to take a closer look. Being baptised should be like a personal revival. I believe a whole church baptised in water and the Spirit would experience a great revival.

Baptism is transformation

Like many people, I was baptised as an infant. I love the truth that God is at work in us even as small babies. I am glad my parents' faith was involved as I was baptised and counted part of the church family. At this time, we were living on the Isle of Gigha in the Inner Hebrides. My family were God-fearing, but not yet fully surrendered to Christ. In 1985, my dad had a powerful encounter with the Lord which changed our family. He was filled with the Spirit and my mum was also set on fire for God. Things progressed quickly and this encounter changed everything for us as a family. Our family were dairy farmers. We had lived in that island community for generations. But in 1987, God called my parents from farming to mission.

I will never forget the farm sale. I was 11 years old. I can remember my mum quietly crying in the kitchen as everything was sold, everything was given up for the sake of Jesus and his call to mission. My parents were going to join The Faith Mission and spread the gospel across the Highlands of Scotland. There would be no secure income, no beautiful farm. We were leaving in obedience to God's call. I remember it so clearly. There was no doubt that Jesus was Lord in our family.

This was the first time I had seen other people saturated with God: my own parents. It made a deep impression on me. We were a normal family, but God came first. My parents went on to spend 25 years in missions work, leading many people to Jesus and serving the Lord wholeheartedly. Their reward will be in heaven. They chose Jesus, not comfort. They chose revival, not a rut.

I believe this witness from my parents sparked a work of God in my own life. A few years later, God filled my life as he had done with my dad. I experienced the baptism of the Spirit as I surrendered my life fully to Jesus and sought a cleansing from sin and empowering by the Spirit.

I can still remember the moment clearly. I felt deeply convicted of my half-hearted Christian experience and was thirsty for God. I remember feeling my great need for God. I hated my sin, but was also worried about what others would think of me if I went forward to the front after the meeting for prayer. I just remember stepping out of the pew into the aisle and someone leading me in a prayer for God's cleansing and filling in my heart. I prayed very simply, but sincerely. Nothing dramatic happened outwardly, but when I got up I knew God had come to me. He had washed me and filled me with the Spirit. That same night I stood up in front of hundreds of other young people to testify to what God had done in me. I went home transformed.

We were attending a Baptist church at the time and I was baptised as an adult at 15 years old. This was the start of a new work of the Spirit in me. God had flooded into my young life and I could not be the same again. My experience of growing up in a number of different churches, with different understandings of baptism, meant I experienced two water baptisms, just for good measure! But, the main thing is that I was born again, genuinely following Jesus and baptised with the Spirit.

Salvation and the power of the Spirit don't leave us dry. We are now chosen, changed and charged with power from heaven. When we ask what revival might look like, baptismal life and power is a pretty good answer.

Baptism with water: new life in Christ

Baptism is a water picture of our salvation and discipleship. Baptism is associated with repentance, dying to self, rising to new life and belonging to Christ. Baptism with water is a mark of God's covenant promise of salvation. God reaches out to us in grace and we respond by faith. Baptism is a sign and sacrament of the new covenant. Baptism reminds us of God redeeming his people from bondage in Egypt and their redemption as they passed through the waters of the Red Sea.

John's baptism was about both repentance and preparation for God's kingdom coming in Jesus. In Matthew 3, God is about to do something new! Jesus identified with sinners, revealed his identity, was an example of obedience and revealed the plan of salvation as he was baptised by John. The account of Jesus' baptism is amazing:

At that time Jesus came from Nazareth in Galilee and was baptised by John in the Jordan. Just as Jesus was coming up out of the water, he saw heaven being torn open and the Spirit descending on him like a dove. And a voice came from heaven: 'You are my Son, whom I love; with you I am well pleased.' At once the Spirit sent him out into the wilderness, and he was in the wilderness forty days, being tempted by Satan. He was with the wild animals, and angels attended him.
(Mark 1.9–13)

Jesus was entering ministry and the role of a suffering servant in the power of the Spirit. His baptism was marked by commissioning, servanthood and sonship. I love the revelation of the Father, Son and Spirit at this baptism. God the Holy Trinity powerfully endorsed the ministry, identity and mission of Jesus. Michael Green points out that in Jesus' baptism we can see him identifying with John's baptism of repentance, then there was his own baptism of the cross and the baptism of the Spirit.[1] We are caught up into all this in baptism.

Baptism reminds us that as Christians we have a relationship with God; a relationship of repentance, cleansing, adoption, faith and intimacy. Baptism is dying to the old sinful nature and rising to new life in Christ. Water symbolises washing sin away. Baptism is an outward sign of an inward faith. Baptism speaks on new birth (John 3.5), washing (1 Cor. 6.11) and new life (Gal. 3.27). As Michael Green said, 'It is like being immersed, sunk into Christ.'[2] This is a sacrament of total commitment, dying and rising with Christ meaning the end of an old life and the start of a new life. Baptism is about full immersion in God. This is what it means to be saturated and soaked in God.

Why be baptised? Jesus was baptised (Matt. 3.13–17). It is a command in the Bible to be baptised (Matt. 28.19; Acts 2.38). It represents an encounter with Jesus. As in Acts 8, we believe first, then are baptised (Acts 8.26–39). It is part of belonging to God's family and church community (1 Cor. 12.12–14). Baptism is a sign of covenantal, eternal and deep relationship with God (Col. 2.11–12).

What does baptism mean? It is a sign of your new life with God (John 3.5) and your love for God. You are spiritually washed and cleansed (1 Cor. 6.11; Acts 22.16). It is a picture of dying and rising with Christ (Col. 2.11–12; Rom. 6.4). This means your old way of life of sin is gone and you die to sin. Then a new life from God is

---

1 M. Green, *Baptism* (Eugene, OR: Wipf & Stock, 1987), p. 43.

2 Green, *Baptism*, p. 47.

given in which you must live from now on. It is a powerful marker of a new life. You are now a follower and disciple of Jesus, no matter what! Baptism also brings you into the worldwide Christian Church (1 Cor. 12.12–14) and commissions you to serve (Matt. 28.16–20).

What does baptism actually do? It's a sign of God's grace towards you and the sign of your faith. It is faith alone that saves, so to be baptised is linked with our faith and trust in Jesus; having become a Christian by repentance and faith, we are baptised as a sign of that faith. This is what Peter teaches:

> . . . to those who were disobedient long ago when God waited patiently in the days of Noah while the ark was being built. In it only a few people, eight in all, were saved through water, and this water symbolises baptism that now saves you also – not the removal of dirt from the body but the pledge of a clear conscience towards God. It saves you by the resurrection of Jesus Christ . . .
> (1 Peter 3.20–21)

Baptism is a deep and profound lifestyle of following Jesus whole-heartedly. A baptised Christian takes time to confess and repent of sin and is committed to walking in freedom from the power of sin. A baptised Christian expects to be fully obedient to God and to be filled with the Spirit. Baptism calls every Christian to serve and engage with the mission of God around them and use their spiritual gifts to serve others.

Baptism celebrates salvation by faith through grace so much and with such abandon, joy and overflowing life that it simply calls us to unreserved devotion to Jesus. We can never be the same when we are right with God. We are saved, justified by faith and have peace with God. This new life in Christ is extraordinary news! God has turned our lives around! Let's mark that wonderful truth and experience with water baptism.

Baptism with the Holy Spirit: power from heaven

As we have seen, water baptism is awesome enough, but after the resurrection of Jesus, the first disciples were about to be utterly transformed by the baptism of the Holy Spirit.

In Acts 1.5 we read Jesus' words to his disciples, 'For John baptised with water, but in a few days you will be baptised with the Holy Spirit.' Then later at Cornelius's house, Peter, seeing the Gentiles receive the Holy Spirit just as in Acts 2 in Jerusalem, says in Acts 11.16, 'Then I remembered what the Lord had said: "John baptised with water, but you will be baptised with the Holy Spirit."'[3]

The baptism in the Holy Spirit that was released at Pentecost remains available and abundant today. We need the baptism of the Spirit today in our churches. It is a baptism of holiness, power, truth and freedom.

It seems clear from Acts 19.2 that, as Martyn Lloyd-Jones said, 'You can be a child of God and yet not be baptised with the Holy Spirit.'[4] Some new believers in the early Church were followers of Jesus, but had not even heard of the Holy Spirit. Peter laid his hands on them and they received the Spirit in power just as at the first day of Pentecost. This is important because everyone needs to seek the baptism, filling and empowering of the Spirit in their own life.

For some this comes through the laying on of hands in prayer ministry. Others find this experience of God's grace in different ways such as confession of sin or simply seeking God for a fresh encounter. Here is one account from a Faith Mission worker, writing to John George Govan, founder of The Faith Mission. He says:

---

3 See Matthew 3.11 and Luke 3.16.

4 D. M. Lloyd-Jones, *Joy Unspeakable* (Eastbourne: Kingsway, 1995), p. 24.

I feel most concerned and deeply exercised about real revival . . . I know personally that I need to get baptised into a new life of power that God may be pleased to use me to bring revival. To this end I am going home to meet my God and shall tell my people the necessity of being alone with Him.[5]

I loved reading the story of how Revd Douglas Brown met God and received the baptism of the Spirit that led to the 1921 revival in East Anglia. He writes:

I thank God for that morning when He nearly broke my heart in my study, and I learnt the meaning of the Baptism of the Holy Ghost for the first time, when I saw all the things that were wrong, and which I could not combat, and I knew that the only hope for usefulness and power and joy and gentleness and love, was for Jesus Christ to absolutely reign in my life. I knelt there with tears running down my cheeks, and I said, 'Lord Jesus, I am not worthy, but O Lord Jesus Thou hast told me, Thou hast led me, Thou hast brought me to this. For the sake of my church, for the sake of men and women that I meet day by day, for the sake of my witness to that wonderful Calvary, Lord Jesus. I ask Thee now and I trust Thee to give me the Holy Spirit. I will receive Him for a life of purity, a life of power, a life of loyalty to Thee, a life of faithful witness. None of these things could ever be mine in my own power. I am a horrible failure.' God gave me the Spirit that morning and I thanked Him for it. That last Sunday I went into the pulpit and a Voice said, 'Whatsoever He saith unto you, do it.' I said, 'Anything Lord.' The Voice said, 'Go down and impel your people to come to Jesus.' I shall never forget that morning as I made my way down from the pulpit. That night

---

5   I. R. Govan, *Spirit of Revival* (Edinburgh: Faith Mission, 1978), p. 181.

96 people came out for Jesus Christ. Within four days I was in Lowestoft, the cloud burst and souls were being born again by the score . . . The preaching was the old-fashioned evangel of God's grace to sinful men.[6]

I love that honest testimony. The baptism of the Spirit is about Jesus reigning truly within our hearts. Duncan Campbell said, 'The baptism of the Holy Spirit is the revelation of Jesus.'[7] Again, this baptism is about Jesus being lifted high, Jesus being at the centre and our lives being empowered to live for his glory.

The simple truth is that the Holy Spirit wants to flood the Church with his gifts, fruit, wisdom and power. This is a baptism of power. Power to pray (Isa. 62.6–7), preach (John 6.63) and serve with signs and wonders (1 Thess. 1.5). The Holy Spirit empowers us to overflow with passion for Jesus (1 Thess. 3.5), to fear God (Ps. 19.12–14), to live a holy life (1 Thess. 5.23) and to have a deep compassion for the lost (Rom. 10.1).

We need this power from the Spirit and the Spirit of revelation to know Jesus better (Phil. 3.10), walk in humility (Jas. 4.10) and practise secret righteousness (Matt. 6). We need the power of the Spirit so we can flow in the gifts of the Spirit (1 Cor. 12—14), especially prophecy and healing. These are all impossible without being saturated with the Spirit. Don't we long to see more of the manifest presence and power of God at work through the Church, through every Christian? If so, we need to pray for every follower of Jesus to be baptised with the Spirit and have the signs of the kingdom of God follow those who believe.

If we are to understand and experience the baptism of the Spirit, we need to receive the Spirit as he is. We will examine the gifts of the Spirit more in later chapters, but I want us to remember that

6 Govan, *Spirit of Revival*, pp. 180–1.
7 D. Campbell, *The Price and Power of Revival* (London: Scripture Illustrations, 1956), p. 16.

much of the ministry of the Spirit has been forgotten today, even in charismatic churches.

In his amazing book, *The Person and Work of the Holy Spirit*, R. A. Torrey sets out the truth that we are to be filled with the Spirit of Christ (Rom. 8.9), Spirit of truth (John 14.16–18), Spirit of holiness (Rom. 1.4), Spirit of judgement and burning (Isa. 4.4), Spirit of wisdom and understanding (Isa. 11.2), Spirit of counsel and might (Isa. 11.2), Spirit of knowledge and the fear of the Lord (Isa. 11.2), Spirit of grace (Heb. 10.29), Spirit of grace and supplication (Zech. 12.10) and the Spirit of glory (1 Pet. 4.14).[8]

We still have so much to learn about the Holy Spirit. We have so much more to encounter and we need his baptism to receive these truths deep into our souls.

The Holy Spirit is:

- Creator (Gen. 1.1–2)
- Teacher (John 14.26; 16.12–14)
- Intercessor (Rom. 8.26–27)
- Comforter (John 14.26)
- Guide (Acts 8)
- Sender (Acts 13.2–4)
- Life Transformer (Eph. 3.14–19)
- Adopter (Rom. 8.15–16)
- Witness to Jesus Christ (John 15.26–27).

The ministry of the Spirit is to glorify Jesus (John 16.14), convict the world of sin (John 16.8–11), bring regeneration (John 3.3–5), impart revelation (Eph. 1.17–18), indwell the believer (Rom. 8.2) and give power to witness (Acts 1.8).

What could revival be like? It looks like the Church being baptised with water and the Spirit so that the world meets Jesus.

---

8   R. A. Torrey, *The Person and Work of the Holy Spirit* (New Kensington, PA: Whitaker House, 1996).

Imagine people being saturated with the Holy Spirit and you will understand revival. The Spirit of God is beyond magnificent. We want to make him most welcome in our lives, homes, churches and communities, so he can fulfil his ministry in all its splendour and we may see Jesus.

Have you received the Holy Spirit? Have you been baptised with God's empowering presence? Are you surrendered to all the Spirit wants to do in and through you?

If not, take some time now and pray through the words of this old hymn. This is the heart we need in the Church of today. I believe the key to the baptism of the Spirit is not only seeking more of God, but giving our all to God.

All to Jesus I surrender,
All to Him I freely give;
I will ever love and trust Him,
In His presence daily live.

I surrender all,
I surrender all.
All to Thee, my blessed Saviour,
I surrender all.

All to Jesus I surrender,
Humbly at His feet I bow;
Worldly pleasures all forsaken,
Take me, Jesus, take me now.

All to Jesus I surrender,
Make me, Saviour, wholly Thine;
Let me feel the Holy Spirit,
Truly knowing Thou art mine.

All to Jesus I surrender,
Lord, I give myself to Thee;
Fill me with Thy love and power,
Let Thy blessing fall on me.

All to Jesus I surrender,
Now I feel the sacred flame.
Oh, the joy of full salvation!
Glory, glory to His name![9]

---

9   J. W. Van DeVenter, 'All to Jesus I Surrender', in *Songs of Victory* (Edinburgh: The Faith Mission, 1998), hymn 607.

Part 3

LEARNING TO LIVE
A GOD-SATURATED
LIFE

How can I cultivate revival in everyday life?

As people and churches, we need to prepare the way, catch the wave and do what it takes to get ready for God to move in power. So what can we do in ordinary life, day by day, to spiritually rehydrate and be filled with God?

We don't just want a flash flood; we want a deep saturation. Revival is a work of the Holy Spirit, yet he is always looking to be outpoured through people who are ready. Revivals don't come out of nowhere. There is a seeking, a deep longing, a discipline of waiting and prayerful watching and crying out. I want to call churches to respond; to see what is possible and to prepare for it. We need churches with a big vision for revival.

How can we move from dehydration to saturation? The remaining chapters are about what we can do to get ready. There are things we can do and values we can seek to live out in order to dive into, drink of and swim in the living water. There is a wave to be caught, if we will seek revival God's way, not our way. God is sovereign in revival, yet we are also responsible for preparing our hearts and following through with commitment.

We don't always appreciate water in a world where we can simply turn on a tap. Water is the most important resource on earth. It is absolutely essential to our survival. A person can live for about a month without food but only days without water. Water is an everyday necessity and little by little our common experience tells us we get better results if we hydrate with water. This has to be regular, daily and is unremarkable. So, we need to find living water in the ordinary unremarkable rhythms of spiritual life. We have to physically drink every day and we also need to come to Christ and spiritually drink every day.

Living out kingdom values every day, in an ordinary, even inconspicuous, way is key. Again, we have to do it every day. To stay saturated, we need to learn how to stay spiritually revived in the ordinary. We need to actually want this water in our lives, homes, churches and communities, even our nation.

What kind of regular lifestyle might promote revival? I believe there are ways we can live, values we can embody, choices we can make and priorities we can act on that will bring streams into the deserts of this world.

Over the coming chapters we will explore how we can make prayer for a fresh move of the Holy Spirit a life priority. It is time to humble ourselves and seek God in prayer. We also want to make more space for the Holy Spirit to move in our churches so people will be saved, healed and set free.

We will need to consider how we learn to make disciples of Jesus in our community. Our passion is to see people come to faith in Christ. We also want to help one another grow in confidence and leadership. We want to learn to seek first his kingdom and engage biblically in the issues facing our world today.

We need to create capacity to revitalise churches and be generous in sending people out to plant the gospel. It is our sending, not seating capacity, that is key! We need prepared leaders with holy habits, walking ancient paths, who are ready for anything!

Another huge issue for us to learn more of and live out more is how we can love each other as a caring church family. Developing a healthy church family takes commitment, time and participation. No church is perfect. We all struggle and need help at times. That is why friendships and real fellowship are so important.

Also, as John Mark Comer puts it:

. . . we must move beyond Sunday Services and a network of loose ties to become a robust counter anti-culture not just against the world, but for the world. Because we're not just against evil, but for good. We're for love, joy, thriving marriages and families, children brought up in loving delight, adults moving off the egocentric operating system to become people of love, true freedom, justice for all and unity in diversity.[1]

This is about pursuing radical holiness and biblical ethical values. We need a bright godliness in our generation that captures the heart of the glory and goodness of God.

There are no shortcuts when we set out to renew the Church and when we pray 'Come, Holy Spirit' with sincerity. If we are serious about taking responsibility as individuals and together for praying for a fresh move of the Spirit, making disciples in our community and loving each other as a church family, it is clear this will call us to a higher level of commitment, sacrifice and generosity, and to a reordering of our priorities. I won't pretend that will be easy. But, I believe it will be worth it.

Jesus calls us to learn to live this way. He rejected the easy route. Dying to self is the way to multiplying and to being saturated with God (John 12.23–28; Gal. 2.20; Matt. 16.24–26; Luke 9.23). Something may need to change in us. What areas might I need to address in my life?

- **How is my relationship with God?** It's time to get to know God through Scripture, prayer, fasting, worshipping and reconciling. Imagine a Church where we all prayed together!
- **Am I a witness for Christ?** It's time to stir that passion, and focus on people who don't yet know Jesus. Imagine a Church where everyone shared the gospel.

---

1 J. M. Comer, *Live No Lies: Recognize and resist the three enemies that sabotage your peace* (London: Form, 2021), p. 231.

- **Am I serving generously?** It's time to discover my spiritual gifts and decide to use them to serve others. Imagine a Church where everyone gave generously and joyfully.
- **Am I helping to build community?** It's time to commit to wholehearted participation on Sundays. Imagine a Church where everyone fully engaged in fellowship and friendship.
- **Am I Spirit-saturated?** It's time for me to ask God to cleanse me and fill me. Imagine a Church where everyone was filled with the Spirit.

It is good to reflect on what belonging to a church in a meaningful and biblical way looks like, and what it means to learn to grow in promoting revival. This means everyone having life-giving spiritual disciplines. This is basic Christianity. We take responsibility for our own Christian lives and the life of the Church together.

We need our discipleship to go deeper than the prevailing culture around us if we are to rebuild and become more spiritually fruitful than before. Can we find simple ways and habits of revival preparation, deepening discipleship and faithfulness to God that will make us spiritually stronger and more able to be equipped for whatever happens? This may be a time of pruning, waiting, growth and multiplying more fruitfully.

Don't make this someone else's responsibility. Don't shift it to other people. If you sense the roaring wave of the Spirit coming, it's time for you to partner, cooperate, obey and follow that leading no matter what.

It is time to learn, time to change, time to adapt, repent and prepare. It is time to get into a saturating routine, a hydrating habit and find new spiritual life in ancient ways. No one can walk this for us. We need to acquire the honesty, courage and discipline to step into learning to prepare for revival.

In the remaining chapters I have suggested eight ancient paths or streams of saturated living we need to recover if we are to see the missing revival emerge:

1 'My soul thirsts for God': *prioritising prayer*
2 'Wash me . . . cleanse me': *hunger for holiness*
3 'A fountain of tears': *loving deeply*
4 'Wells of salvation': *sharing Jesus*
5 'There is a river': *encountering God*
6 'A well-watered garden': *living for the kingdom*
7 'I will pour out my Spirit on all people': *everyone overflowing*
8 'When you pass through the waters': *embracing the cost*

How can we cultivate revival in everyday life? One of these days, someone will do it. It has happened time and again, just not in our lifetime and in our communities. God will move extraordinarily. But, it won't be an accident. Someone, somewhere will pay the price of having learned to fear God above all else, fully obey the Spirit and surrender everything to Christ. God keeps his promises. When the conditions for revival have been met, he will come.

I want to be around when that happens. Don't you?

7

'My soul thirsts for God':
prioritising prayer

As the deer pants for streams of water,
so my soul pants for you, my God.
My soul thirsts for God, for the living God.
When can I go and meet with God?
(Psalm 42.1–2)

There has never been a revival without prayer. It is as simple as that. So why is there so little prayer in our lives and our churches? We do not have because we do not ask.

Praying people are thirsty. I love prayer meetings with spiritually thirsty people, crying out for floods on the dry ground. Prayer is drinking the living water. We must give ourselves to waiting upon God in prayer. There can be no revival without prayer.

In Psalm 42 we see someone desperate for streams of living water, thirsty and panting after God. There is a passion, an eagerness and an intensity of desire for God. Once again we see the powerful image of thirst for God as for streams of water.

Do we want to be saturated with God? This passion is seen throughout Scripture and history. People have longed for more of God and to see his kingdom come in power, transforming lives. Fundamentally it begins when we are thirsty for God himself. David knew this thirst and expressed it often in the Psalms. He longed for God, to be saturated with God. This was his experience and it was lived out in worship, prayer, struggles, questions, lament, failure, restoration and renewed passion. This thirst is something we need today and we need it to be persistent and powerful. Not a fleeing, wistful nostalgia, but a deep ache in our souls for more of God. Something that will draw us to our knees again, so that somehow we might find ourselves living in times of revival once more.

Prayer is sadly neglected

However, let's be honest about our relationship to prayer in churches today. What is the role of prayer in seeing local churches change nations?

I believe we need to see prayer differently so we can unlock its purpose and power. So much prayer is focused on ourselves and our felt needs. We attend to the desires of time, not the needs of eternity. There is no special gift of prayer for people who are 'into prayer' which lets everyone else off.

Why is the prayer meeting so unloved? Perhaps those who don't pray are content with the status quo. The perception may be that prayer is formal, boring, hard work, someone else's job or a specialist activity. Perhaps there may be the feeling that it doesn't work, takes too long or is too spiritually intense. There must be a reason why people often prefer to party rather than pray. The church BBQ is more popular than the church prayer meeting. Somehow many good people in good churches have got the idea that prayer is not 'their thing'. They leave it to other 'more spiritual' people. There is an acute lack of confidence, a sense of insignificance or impotence that cripples getting anywhere in prayer.

We need to recover a sense of what prayer is for and what prayer does! Why pray at all? I often remember reading the challenging words of Leonard Ravenhill, 'No man is greater than his prayer life . . . The secret of praying is praying in secret.'[1] He is right.

---

1 L. Ravenhill, *Why Revival Tarries* (Bloomington, MN: Bethany Fellowship, 1959), pp. 7–8.

We need to learn to work on exercising our weak prayer muscles. There is no such thing as a gift of prayer. Prayer is for everyone. Prayer is simply being in conversation with God. It is intimacy with Jesus. Prayer is the outworking of an actual living relationship with God. Prayer is the most wonderful privilege we have: to relate to God Almighty! The main reason prayer meetings are perceived to be boring is because the private place of prayer is dry.

How many churches do you know with a deep emphasis on prayer? Is it any wonder that years come and go without revival power? Our trust has been in tried and tested methods, budgets, numbers attending, franchise courses, the latest worship songs, relevant teaching and so much else. And all the while we fail to address the crisis of prayerlessness. Why do we believe we can plant and grow churches without prioritising prayer?

Speaking about the climate crisis, Greta Thunberg said this: 'I want you to act as you would in a crisis. I want you to act as if your house is on fire, because it is.'[2] I think she speaks eloquently here in a way we can also apply to the Church and prayer. We need to act as if our spiritual house is on fire. Only God can save the nation and he always uses praying people.

Leonard Ravenhill described the prayer meeting as the Cinderella of the Church: unloved, unsought for.[3] Where are the churches with a real emphasis on prayer? Prayer meetings are the smallest meetings and often have to be revamped to get any interest. Something is missing.

Prayer meetings changed my life

We all know good preachers, but it was good prayer meetings that changed my life. It has been knowing praying people that has

---

2 G. Thunberg, *No One Is Too Small to Make a Difference* (London: Penguin, 2019), pp. 14–15.

3 Ravenhill, *Why Revival Tarries*, p. 1.

had the biggest impact on me. I will never forget prayer meetings with people who knew God intimately. No one had to make those meetings interesting or entertaining. We didn't need gimmicks or activities to keep our interest. Something spiritually flowed from their heart into my heart by my just listening to and learning from these praying men and women.

In the Baptist church I went to in my high school years, I will always remember the Thursday night prayer meeting; spending time listening to men and women crying out to God. This was where I first prayed out loud myself and where I learned from others the art of calling on the name of the Lord.

I love to recall packed student prayer meetings at university as we called on God together, losing track of time and passionately seeking God for our university town of St Andrews in Scotland. There we had half-nights of prayer for revival. We were thirsty and didn't need to be entertained. We were following hard after God.

I will never forget listening to the South African preacher Colin Peckham, as he spoke about prayer. I can still see him urging us to 'get right through to God' in prayer. Not just saying a few words and then moving on, but waiting, persisting, knocking on heaven's door and interceding with energy, vision and passion. This made a very deep impact on me. I could see they had something I didn't have in the place of prayer, and I wanted it. Prayer meetings are not overly popular at the moment, but God is there. Isn't that what really matters?

Prayer becoming our priority

What is going on behind the scenes? If we are serious about walking with God, we thirst to go deeper and move past the shallow places of prayer.

What would happen if we changed our priorities and put prayer much higher up the list, or even made it the top priority? We would see more Christians who really knew how to pray even without a crisis. I think we would become much deeper Christians. I imagine there would be much more love, more supernatural power from the Spirit at work. I am sure we would be hearing more from God and be more led by the Spirit. Also, wouldn't we simply see more prayers answered? It is amazing just to think on it for a while. What would happen if we prayed as our top priority? We have tried so much to spark our churches into life, but we haven't really yet tried God.

Something I believe we need today is a vision of becoming a praying Church. Prayerful people are amazing. I love meeting people who have a depth in God. They inspire me to much more in my own relationship with Jesus. People of prayer are marked by humility, intimacy, tenderness and compassion. They know the value of the presence of God and they thirst to stay there. Such people also make an impact on others around them in the power of the Spirit. Duncan Campbell writes about one such woman he met:

> I could take you to a little cottage in the Hebrides and intro-
> duce you to a young woman. She is not educated; one could
> not say that she was polished in the sense that we use the
> word, but I have known that young woman to pray heaven
> into a community, to pray power into a meeting. I have known
> her to be so caught in the power of the Holy Ghost that men
> and women around her trembled – not influence, but power.[4]

We need more such people today in every church and community. The revival in England in 1859 was partly due to the preaching and ministry of Charles Spurgeon, who commented on meeting a similar praying people:

---

4   R. Hession, *The Calvary Road* (London: CLC, 1974), p. 45.

When I came to New Park Street Chapel it was but to a handful of people to whom I first preached, yet I could never forget how earnestly they prayed. Sometimes they seemed to plead as though they could really see the Angel of the Covenant with them, and as if they must have a blessing from Him. More than one we were all so awe-struck with the solemnity of the meeting that we sat silently for some moments while the Lord's Power appeared to overshadow us and all I could do on such occasions was to pronounce the benediction and say, 'Dear friends, we have had the Spirit of God very manifestly with us tonight. Let us go home and take care not to lose His gracious influence.' Then down came the blessing; the house was filled with hearers and many souls were saved.[5]

The Church was birthed in a prayer meeting and I believe God wants the Church how he started it. What will it take for us to get more serious about prayer, revival and depending on the Spirit? Is powerlessness in mission related to our patchy prayer life as a Church? What might happen if we caught a fresh vision of being a praying Church? We currently don't seem to prioritise prayer as we could. Why is that? How can we be an Acts 1 Church that receives power when we pray? We have much to learn and work on. One thing is very clear: if we want to see revival, we absolutely need to pray.

It is possible to pray

I believe that the Holy Spirit is putting a fresh desire in his people to pray. Even though we have much to learn, it is possible that we can become the prayer-saturated Church our nation needs. It won't be easy. There are no shortcuts. It will take vision, passion, patience

---

5   B. H. Edwards, *Revival: A people saturated with God* (Darlington: Evangelical Press, 1990), p. 78.

and persistence. As E. M. Bounds said, 'Prayer has no substitutes.'[6] There is no other way.

If only all God's people would say, 'I am an intercessor.' This is a ministry for everyone, just like evangelism and loving our neighbour; we are all intercessors and prayer-warriors. Prayer is putting God to work and is for absolutely everyone.

Revivals are usually marked by powerful and soul-searching preaching, the conviction of sin and emphasis on conversion to Christ. There is also always a deep dependence on the power of prayer. It was said of Charles Finney, the American revivalist, that 'preaching and praying were his only weapons'. Having spent a day in prayer, he wrote of 'a day of an unspeakable agony and wrestling in my soul'.[7] Reading one account of revival in Wales in 1859, we learn that, 'The people cannot think of anything but to feed their cattle and attend prayer meetings.'[8] In a similar story of the Lewis Revival of 1949–53, one commentator remarked, 'It didn't matter what you were doing. You were just longing for the prayer meeting.'[9]

An incredible example of powerful praying was on the Isle of Bernera during a Communion Season in 1952. The hard spiritual atmosphere was so obvious that Duncan Campbell stopped preaching halfway through his sermon:

Just then he noticed the boy visibly moved with a burden for souls. He thought, 'That boy is in touch with God and living nearer to the Saviour than I am.' So leaning over the pulpit he said: 'Donald will you lead us in prayer'. That dear lad rose to his feet and in his prayer made reference to Revelation chapter 4, 'O God, I seem to be gazing through the open door. I see

6 E. M. Bounds, *E. M. Bounds on Prayer* (Grand Rapids, MI: Baker Books, 1990), p. 317.

7 W. Duewel, *Revival Fire*, pp. 112–13.

8 Duewel, *Revival Fire*, p. 165.

9 Edwards, *Revival*, p. 256.

the Lamb in the midst of the Throne, with the keys of death and Hell at His girdle.' He began to sob, then lifting his eyes toward heaven cried, 'O God, there is power there, let it loose.' With the force of a hurricane the Spirit of God swept into the building and the floodgates opened. The church resembled a battlefield. On one side many were prostrated and weeping; on the other side some threw their arms into the air crying. God had come.[10]

Our generation in the UK has never known revival and has never known such revival praying. But, it is possible in our day and in our time. In Luke 11.1 we read, 'Lord, teach us to pray.' Not teach us to preach or teach us to do miracles. Everything flowed from prayer; authority, grace, love, compassion, wisdom, signs and wonders – all flowed from prayer.

There is a vacancy at this time in the Church for praying men and women. Who will answer the call? God is searching for people to stand in the gap. It won't happen overnight. We build in prayer over time. We can build our prayer muscles, just like we go to the gym. But, it is possible to pray. In James 5.17–18, we are reminded of a praying man who was as normal as anyone else:

Elijah was a human being, even as we are. He prayed earnestly that it would not rain, and it did not rain on the land for three and a half years. Again he prayed, and the heavens gave rain, and the earth produced its crops.

It is possible to pray and see God move. We need to see that this can and will happen. Remember that throughout history, God has placed his hand on people in extraordinary ways, and made them men and women of prayer:

10 Edwards, *Revival*, p. 13.

- Abraham pleaded with God over a whole city (Gen. 18)
- Jacob wrestled with God, and was never the same again (Gen. 32)
- Moses interceded with God, and saved a rebellious people (Exod. 32)
- Hannah wept with God, and God raised up a prophet (1 Sam. 1)
- Elijah worked with God to bring revival (1 Kings 18).

Most of all, Jesus was a man of prayer. In Mark 1.35, it says:

> Very early in the morning, while it was still dark, Jesus got up, left the house and went off to a solitary place, where he prayed.

The prayer life of Jesus is all over the gospel accounts. I guess that isn't a major surprise. But perhaps what is more surprising is that the disciples, who seemed not to be so great at prayer in Matthew 26, in the garden of Gethsemane, where they slept rather than prayed multiple times – even they became people of prayer. It is possible to pray. The power for prayer in the early Church came when Jesus commanded them not to leave Jerusalem in Acts 1. They started their ministry in active prayer, waiting and thirsting for God to send his Spirit. Even though the Spirit came 'suddenly' in Acts 2, it was not a surprise. They had been praying, expecting and waiting on God for exactly that. Their first lesson after Jesus ascended was in making prayer their priority.

I believe the Spirit of God is planting a heart for prayer in his people today. He is raising up an army of praying people. We are learners, but we are thirsty and want to grow in prayer. Here are a few ways we can prioritise the kind of prayer we will need to see for God to saturate our land again:

1 We start by repenting of prayerlessness and committing ourselves to prioritising prayer and planning to pray (Neh. 1.4–7).

2 Dealing with sin is so important. Pray Psalm 51 and ask God for a clean heart, so he can fill you with his Spirit of prayer.

3 Simply get alone with God even for 20–30 minutes a day and spend some time both listening and talking with him. Getting to know his presence and his voice. You can increase the time as you are led by the Spirit and according to your capacity.

4 Start at home. Let your home become a house of prayer. Prayer-saturated homes are vital in any move of God.

5 Call your church to prayer (Joel 2.12). If your church has a prayer meeting, make every effort to go and envision others to go. If you don't have such a meeting, see about starting one either in church or in your home.

6 Encourage others around you to pray. Many people have never seen a prayer life modelled to them. You could be someone who helps another believer discover the power of prayer. Meeting to pray with others is so encouraging. So many people find it easier to pray with others than alone.

7 Don't stop praying. If you ebb and flow, don't be discouraged. If you stop for any reason, don't dwell on it or give up because you feel a failure. Get straight back into prayer. We all have seasons where we feel like giving up and sometimes do. Just keep going and start again.

That last point is very important. In my own story I have had countless times when I have given up because I just felt a failure. I have often struggled feeling my own inadequacy in prayer. I set myself a high bar and don't often meet it, so get discouraged. It makes me feel vulnerable to share, but this is a big deal for me. At the conference where I recommitted myself to prayer, I really felt something shift, but I knew that in a few weeks I would be struggling again to pray. All I can say is, I am so grateful that God is the God of all grace. He never drives anyone away who comes to him (John 6.37). I know I am called to prayer. When I am weak, I know God is so gracious and I just need to get back on track with him and keep going. By God's grace, I won't ever stop praying.

'God comes where people want him'

At a recent New Wine United conference, Jon Tyson shared his insight into his studies in revivals and how they start. It really struck me as so true. He simply said, 'God comes where people want him.' I believe there is no better way of wanting God than by prayer.

Lord, I want you in my life. I have been praying this prayer more and more recently, just walking along the street or doing something mundane and praying this prayer. I want to welcome Jesus into my life. To want Jesus more than TV, phones or social media or any other addiction. I want him to take my hand and lead me. I want to welcome him and I want him in my life in every part.

Lord, I want you in my home. I grew up knowing the family prayer altar in my home. We do need God in our homes, in marriage and parenting. We need God around our kitchen tables and in every part of our homes. Our children and young people need to see God in their home life. God, I welcome you into my home. This was Joshua's prayer in Joshua 24.15, 'As for me and my household, we will serve the LORD.'

Lord, I want you in my church. We can't just assume that God is welcome in churches. We have welcomed so much that should not be welcomed, such as identity politics, into churches. Now is the time for us to want God in our churches again. Welcoming his presence and power back into our church community and life. Oh God, we need you and we want you in our church.

Lord, I want you in my region. At a time when culture is getting rid of Jesus, I want to welcome him in my region and culture. God is welcome in Loughton and Epping Forest. Lord, you are welcome in my local area and in my nation. In every sphere of life, including education, business, media, sport, music, the internet, technology, science, nature and every other sphere; we want God to move. Prayer is welcoming Jesus everywhere.

We pray until something happens. I learned to pray from saturated people. It was caught more than taught. We pray streams into deserts, hope into despair and healing into pain. We pray light into darkness, joy into suffering, peace into struggle and revival into dry bones.

You don't have to persuade a thirsty person to drink. We started this chapter with the thirst of Psalm 42. Verse 2 says, 'When can I go and meet with God?' This is the ache of anyone who wants more of God. We are drawn instinctively to prayer. Going to meet God is what prayer is all about.

It's up to us just how spiritually dehydrated or saturated we are. Those who prioritise prayer will be saturated with God.

8

'Wash me . . . cleanse me':
hunger for holiness

Have mercy on me, O God,
  according to your unfailing love;
according to your great compassion
  blot out my transgressions.
Wash away all my iniquity
  and cleanse me from my sin.
For I know my transgressions,
  and my sin is always before me.
Against you, you only, have I sinned
  and done what is evil in your sight;
so you are right in your verdict
  and justified when you judge.
Surely I was sinful at birth,
  sinful from the time my mother conceived me.
Yet you desired faithfulness even in the womb;
  you taught me wisdom in that secret place.
Cleanse me with hyssop, and I shall be clean;
  wash me, and I shall be whiter than snow.
(Psalm 51.1–7)

Do you know any people you would describe as holy? Why is it so rare to know such people? We know funny people, generous people, gifted people . . . but holy people?

What makes holy people different is not that they follow rules, but that they are overflowing in their relationship with God. As

Duncan Campbell said, 'That is the secret of holiness, not my holiness but his. Jesus empty me and fill me with Your holiness to the brim.'[1] Holy people are filled to the brim with Jesus. Isn't that a beautiful way to live? I have met holy people and I long to be like them, because they are like Jesus.

Of any scripture, Psalm 51 has probably had the greatest impact on me as a prayer I pray knowing my need for washing, cleansing and revival in my own life. I resonate so deeply with David in his conviction of sin, thirst for cleansing and desire to get right with God.

Holiness really matters

We have become overwhelmed by life but underwhelmed by God, resulting in careless living. We can be content to condone sin, rather than come for cleansing. Sometimes the Church even seems to resist holiness as though it were throwing off some bygone concept. We need to stop resisting holiness as something suspicious, scornful, optional, negative and legalistic.

In 1 Peter 1.16, God says through Peter, 'Be holy, because I am holy.' There is such a great need for a fresh baptism of God's holiness. Such holiness is so far removed from our caricatures. Holiness is a glorious work of grace, a perfecting of love and an experience of the Spirit.

Why is holiness unattractive to the contemporary Church? We can be shy to talk about being holy, in case we appear judgemental, narrow-minded or overly traditional. We are too well discipled in selfishness and 'me-culture'. Why don't we want to be holy and why do we seem more nervous of holiness than sinfulness? We want power, but do we want purity?

God is not a tool for getting our needs met. We talk about heaven invading earth, but sometimes we love earth too much. There is no

---

1 D. Campbell, *The Price and Power of Revival* (London: Scripture Illustrations, 1956), p. 35.

cross for us. Jesus has to do all the dying in our self-centred gospel. We badly need to repent of self-sufficiency, self-reliance and self-salvation (Isa. 30.10–15).

How we live matters to God. Holiness matters! We are called to righteousness. Jesus walked in dark places with purity. If we care about exercising and experiencing spiritual power, authority and honouring God, we must care about holiness. For me, holiness starts with a fresh vision of God as he really is and ourselves as we really are. After this we can never be the same again.

This is a call for the Church to get right with God afresh. A call to conviction of sin, repentance, forgiveness and true freedom. Oswald J. Smith asked, 'Where is the conviction of sin we used to know?'[2] He says, 'In the modern campaign, the evangelist calls upon people to accept Christ, and rightly so. But oh that we could hear sinners calling upon Christ to accept them.'[3] Revival in 1907 in Korea was deeply marked by conviction of sin, with eyewitnesses describing scenes of weeping, confession and crying to God for mercy. A western missionary recalled, 'Every man forgot every other. Each was face to face with God. I can hear yet that fearful sound of hundreds of men pleading with God for life, for mercy.'[4]

We need to be cleansed, washed and purified – all water images – so we can be renewed and revived. We need to pray, but we also need to turn from our wicked ways, so God can heal our land. We read in 2 Chronicles 7.14:

if my people, who are called by my name, will humble themselves and pray and seek my face and turn from their wicked ways, then I will hear from heaven, and I will forgive their sin and will heal their land.

---

2 O. J. Smith, *The Passion for Souls* (Lakeland: The Chaucer Press, 1983), p. 14.

3 Smith, *The Passion for Souls*, p. 45.

4 B. H. Edwards, *Revival: A people saturated with God* (Darlington: Evangelical Press, 1990), pp. 115–16.

This is a promise of whole communities and cities getting into right relationship with God, turning away from sin and walking in holiness.

A clean heart

Holiness is an experience of grace when we connect with the Holy One. This is being in right relationship with God, cleansed from sin and filled with perfect love. This is the intimacy, beauty and depth of holiness. It is relational, not regulatory. Holiness is all about the life of Jesus displayed in us; the works of the kingdom and the character of the King.

I love the description of a clean heart. As Psalm 51 describes, we are washed and cleansed by the Lord when we call upon his mercy. We can know the blessing of a clean heart, a washed conscience and a cleansed soul. There is a cleansing and victory over sin. This is not to say we can be sinless, but we can be victorious through the cleansing and wonder-working power of the blood of Jesus.

The founder of The Faith Mission, John George Govan, often used to preach on the subject of the clean heart. Here is part of his personal testimony as he shared it in 1885. Even though it is from more than a century ago, I find his words still resonate with me very deeply:

I found that the complete giving up of self was to flesh and blood a hard thing to do, and for a time I was not altogether willing to be crucified to the world and have the flesh with all its affections crucified. I discovered then that I cared a good deal of other people's opinion, and lived a great deal for my own glory. But at length I was led to trust the Lord to save me to the uttermost from all sin, and to take away the desires to live for anything else but His glory. I saw from Ephesians 3:17, Revelation 3:20 and John 14:23 that there was a coming of the

119

King Himself to reign in the cleansed hearts of His children.
So, I yielded my heart to its rightful King . . . Since then my life
in Christ has been quite different to what it was before. There
has been such a sense of His continual presence . . . Of course,
there is always temptation from without, but there is victory
because He is within.[5]

I love John George Govan's description that, 'I yielded my heart to
its rightful King.' I have meditated on that phrase over some time
and have adopted it as my own prayer. Is this not the beauty of holiness; a wholehearted yielding of ourselves to God? We are to imitate
the 'lamb-like nature of the Lord Jesus' if we want to experience the
power of the blood. This is the broken, yielded, surrendered disposi-
tion of the Lamb.[6]

This is also the language of Ephesians 5 as Paul calls us to 'follow
God's example' just like Jesus, who 'gave himself up for us', then
goes on to describe a holy, pure and clean heart and lifestyle, which
contrasts so much with our own sinful culture:

Follow God's example, therefore, as dearly loved children
and live a life of love, just as Christ loved us and gave
himself up for us as a fragrant offering and sacrifice to God.
But among you there must not be even a hint of sexual
immorality, or of any kind of impurity, or of greed, because
these are improper for God's holy people. Nor should there
be obscenity, foolish talk or coarse joking, which are out of
place, but rather thanksgiving. For of this you can be sure:
no immoral, impure or greedy person – such a person is
an idolater – has any inheritance in the kingdom of Christ
and of God. Let no one deceive you with empty words, for

---

5   I. R. Govan, *Spirit of Revival* (Edinburgh: Faith Mission, 1978), p. 27.

6   R. Hession, *The Calvary Road* (London: CLC, 1974), p. 56.

because of such things God's wrath comes on those who are disobedient. Therefore do not be partners with them. For you were once darkness, but now you are light in the Lord. Live as children of light (for the fruit of the light consists in all goodness, righteousness and truth) and find out what pleases the Lord. Have nothing to do with the fruitless deeds of darkness, but rather expose them. It is shameful even to mention what the disobedient do in secret. But everything exposed by the light becomes visible – and everything that is illuminated becomes a light. This is why it is said:

'Wake up, sleeper,
   rise from the dead,
   and Christ will shine on you.'

Be very careful, then, how you live – not as unwise but as wise, making the most of every opportunity, because the days are evil. Therefore do not be foolish, but understand what the Lord's will is. Do not get drunk on wine, which leads to debauchery. Instead, be filled with the Spirit, speaking to one another with psalms, hymns, and songs from the Spirit. Sing and make music from your heart to the Lord, always giving thanks to God the Father for everything, in the name of our Lord Jesus Christ.
(Ephesians 5.1–20)

What an amazing call to holiness and the filling of the Spirit. Take a few moments to read over it again. There is a simplicity, honesty and directness here and a real valuing of goodness, righteousness and truth. There is an urgency to separate from wickedness and to be consecrated to God. Paul calls us to 'Live as children of light', '. . . find out what pleases the Lord', and 'Be very careful . . . how you live'. The key to it all is in the filling with the Spirit. Once again, the key is to be saturated with God!

The Scriptures are packed with the call to a clean heart. In Hebrews 10.19–22 we read:

> Therefore, brothers and sisters, since we have confidence to enter the Most Holy Place by the blood of Jesus, by a new and living way opened for us through the curtain, that is, his body, and since we have a great priest over the house of God, let us draw near to God with a sincere heart and with the full assurance that faith brings, having our hearts sprinkled to cleanse us from a guilty conscience and having our bodies washed with pure water.

The writer of Hebrews uses beautiful language of having your 'heart sprinkled' in a work of cleansing by the blood of Jesus and being washed with God's pure water. This is the finished work of salvation, won for us on the cross by the Lord Jesus Christ. His blood can cleanse every stain of sin. His blood goes deeper than any blemish can go.

Ezekiel also prophesies this truth in Ezekiel 36.25. He declares, 'I will sprinkle clean water on you, and you will be clean; I will cleanse you from all your impurities and from all your idols.' God wants to bring cleansing to his people. Psalm 24.3 says, 'Who may ascend the mountain of the LORD? Who may stand in his holy place? The one who has clean hands and a pure heart . . .' Only one thing is holding us back: our sin. Only one antidote can fully deal with sin: the blood of Christ.

Leaders of revival over the years have always carried this heart of holiness. The American revival leader Charles Finney was powerfully used by God in awakenings in the nineteenth century. The messages of repentance and holiness were prominent in his teaching on how to promote a revival. In Finney's *Lectures on Revivals of Religion*, published in 1868, he lists specific areas for Christians to exercise repentance and penitence within, so as to promote holiness of life.[7] This has been described in more recent years as the 'Finney List', which includes: ingratitude, lack of love, neglect of the Bible, unbelief, neglect of prayer, neglect of the means of grace, lying, lack of care for the lost, neglect of family, pride, envy, worldly-mindedness, a critical spirit and a bad temper. It is worth taking some time to look at Finney's list. He took repentance seriously and he actually saw revival. Perhaps there is a lesson there for us. I am sure we could all add more to his list such as prejudice, lack of care for creation or a litany of addictions in postmodern life that Finney could not have conceived of.

The point is that it is healthy to reflect on the obstacles and barriers in us to possessing a clean heart. This is not morbid introspection. It is allowing God to search us and deal with the dark shadows underneath our mild exteriors. We probably all need a deeper cleansing than we know. The intents, attitudes, strongholds and hidden motivations of our hearts and minds need to be brought under the gracious purity and power of the blood of Jesus, for full and free cleansing.

John Wesley had a similar set of questions to Finney. Again, Wesley saw remarkable revival in England and across the UK and American colonies in the eighteenth century. These are 22 questions the members of John Wesley's 'Holy Club' asked themselves every day in their private devotions over 200 years ago:[8]

1 Am I consciously or unconsciously creating the impression that I am better than I really am? In other words, am I a hypocrite?
2 Am I honest in all my acts and words, or do I exaggerate?
3 Do I confidentially pass on to another what was told to me in confidence?
4 Can I be trusted?

---

7 C. G. Finney, *Lectures on Revivals of Religion* (Classic Christian Book.com), pp. 21–27.
8 www.umcdiscipleship.org/resources/everyday-disciples-john-wesleys-22-questions

5 Am I a slave to dress, friends, work, or habits?

6 Am I self-conscious, self-pitying, or self-justifying?

7 Did the Bible live in me today?

8 Do I give it time to speak to me every day?

9 Am I enjoying prayer?

10 When did I last speak to someone else about my faith?

11 Do I pray about the money I spend?

12 Do I get to bed on time and get up on time?

13 Do I disobey God in anything?

14 Do I insist upon doing something about which my conscience is uneasy?

15 Am I defeated in any part of my life?

16 Am I jealous, impure, critical, irritable, touchy, or distrustful?

17 How do I spend my spare time?

18 Am I proud?

19 Do I thank God that I am not as other people, especially as the Pharisees who despised the publican?

20 Is there anyone whom I fear, dislike, disown, criticise, hold a resentment toward or disregard? If so, what am I doing about it?

21 Do I grumble or complain constantly?

22 Is Christ real to me?

When I read through these questions, I hear the heart of Wesley and his friends, not to condemn, but for purity with conviction. These questions are just what the Bible calls us to and we need to take the time to align our hearts with God's Word, not the spirit of the age. Hudson Taylor said, 'God gives His Holy Spirit, not to those who long for Him, not to those who pray for Him, not to those who desire to be filled always; He gives His Spirit to those who obey (Acts 5.32).'[9] We need to get right with God to get saturated with God. Holiness matters because God does care how we live.

---

9 Campbell, *Price and Power of Revival*, p. 36.

Just in case we are tempted to think Finney and Wesley were a bit extreme in searching their hearts so intently, let's read the apostle Peter's approach to holiness:

Therefore, with minds that are alert and fully sober, set your hope on the grace to be brought to you when Jesus Christ is revealed at his coming. As obedient children, do not conform to the evil desires you had when you lived in ignorance. But just as he who called you is holy, so be holy in all you do; for it is written: 'Be holy, because I am holy.' Since you call on a Father who judges each person's work impartially, live out your time as foreigners here in reverent fear. For you know that it was not with perishable things such as silver or gold that you were redeemed from the empty way of life handed down to you from your ancestors, but with the precious blood of Christ, a lamb without blemish or defect. He was chosen before the creation of the world, but was revealed in these last times for your sake. Through him you believe in God, who raised him from the dead and glorified him, and so your faith and hope are in God. Now that you have purified yourselves by obeying the truth so that you have sincere love for each other, love one another deeply, from the heart. For you have been born again, not of perishable seed, but of imperishable, through the living and enduring word of God . . . Therefore, rid yourselves of all malice and all deceit, hypocrisy, envy, and slander of every kind. Like newborn babies, crave pure spiritual milk, so that by it you may grow up in your salvation, now that you have tasted that the Lord is good.
(1 Peter 1.13–23; 2.1–3)

'To be filled we must be cleansed'[10]

We need a deep cleansing in the blood of the Lamb, the Lord Jesus Christ. We need his sin-cleansing, peace-giving, life-imparting power.[11]

The good news is that according to 1 John 1.9, 'If we confess our sins, he is faithful and just and will forgive us our sins and purify us from all unrighteousness.' In this verse John calls for a 'frank, full confession prompted by a true heart repentance'.[12] Paul does the same in 2 Corinthians 7.1: 'Therefore, since we have these promises, dear friends, let us purify ourselves from everything that contaminates body and spirit, perfecting holiness out of reverence for God.'

The times we live in call for us to be sober-minded, eternity-conscious, fully yielded and living distinctively. Do not conform to this sin-sick culture. Be holy in all you do! We don't belong to the world. Holiness comes through the precious blood of Christ. The blood of Christ cleanses from the foulest sin. By faith, we apply the blood of Christ to our hearts. We have a responsibility to be holy; in fact we partner with God in holiness. We do this through responding in obedience and love. Come as you are right now. If we want to be saturated, we need to be cleansed. We can pray as David prayed, 'Create in me a pure heart, O God' (Ps. 51.10). We can receive mercy, grace and holiness.

If you know you are not right with God, don't delay. The power of the cleansing blood is the way to living in the presence of God. As Duncan Campbell wrote, 'The power, the dynamic of a God-possessed personality. Let that loose and revival is at the door. A baptism of holiness, a demonstration of godly living is the crying need of our day . . . Get rightly related to Me!'[13]

---

10 R. Paxson, *Rivers of Living Water* (Edinburgh: Oliphants, 1964), p. 73.

11 Hession, *The Calvary Road*, p. 53.

12 Paxson, *Rivers of Living Water*, p. 70.

13 Campbell, *Price and Power of Revival*, p. 31.

9

'A fountain of tears': *loving deeply*

Oh, that my head were a spring of water
and my eyes a fountain of tears!
I would weep day and night
. for the slain of my people.

Let them come quickly
and wail over us
till our eyes overflow with tears
and water streams from our eyelids.
(Jeremiah 9.1, 18)

I don't usually like to cry. I find it difficult, embarrassing, and I pull tears in quickly so as not to attract attention to the fact that I am crying. I find tears make me very vulnerable.

Jeremiah was a weeping prophet because he served a weeping God. He described the loving thirst he had for God to move among his people producing a 'fountain of tears'. Tears are often a feature of revival associated with deep love, repentance, contrition and also a prayer burden for those still outside Christ.

This is a time to weep, as did Jeremiah, Hannah, Joel, Jesus, Paul, David, Ezra, Job, Micah, Nehemiah and Peter. Our God is so overflowing and saturated with love for everyone in this lost world. His heart breaks with everlasting love. Anyone who comes into living contact with God's heart of love can't help but be deeply moved.

Why this focus on tears? Genuine tears are a beautiful picture of love, compassion, empathy, deep concern, passion, prayer and authenticity. This is not something mechanical or dispassionate; it is genuine love. The language of tears can't be taught, only caught. There are no Bible college courses on weeping, or home-group study series on sobbing. Surely it comes down to love, compassion, empathy, depth of walking with others in the way of Jesus and the cost of following him and seeing others not follow him.

This is a call to heartfelt and persistent love; weeping for our communities, brokenness and compassion. William Booth wrote to one of his officers, urging them to 'try tears' when the work was hard.[1] There is much to weep for, yet our eyes are often too dry.

This time calls for a true compassion for the lost, last and least. Revival is about love and loving people in our communities so much that we will pray, serve, surrender and sacrifice for them. This is a call away from comfort into compassion. We have been consumer Christians, and we are called to be consecrated Christians. The theme of tears is a rich one in Scripture. Tears are a deep sign of love and that we love our communities and can't stand by to see them broken and lost. We need tears today and to recover passion for mission and seeing people saved, healed and delivered. Revival will be birthed in love, tears, prayer and God's vision of a lost world in our hearts. The core of revival is loving deeply.

The school of tears

We have not had many weeping mentors who have helped us learn in the school of tears. I would not associate the contemporary Church with tear-stained ministry. Yet the world weeps every day. People in poverty weep. People who are isolated, grieving, sick or dying know the reality of wet eyes and broken hearts. What does it mean to have the compassion of Jesus? We have so much to learn about moving in deeper compassion.

---

1 L. Ravenhill, *Why Revival Tarries* (Bloomington, MN: Bethany Fellowship, 1959), p. 38.

The school of tears is really about learning to love. Surely this is our great need today and the lesson everything else springs from: loving deeply. Knowing what we know and whom we know, wouldn't tears be the common language of the Church in a broken world? Are our dry eyes a sign of barrenness and hardness?

The Bible is full of love and saturated with tears. It seems God's people really care about God's glory and the suffering around them. All this weeping was about love. Here are just a few examples:

- Jesus lamented over a rebellious Jerusalem (Luke 13.34)
- Paul was a man who served the Lord with tears (Acts 20.18–20)
- Job wept for the poor and needy (Job 30.25)
- Josiah wept and prayed for his people (2 Kings 22.19)
- Ezra wept in repentance as he realised the great sin of his people (Ezra 10.1–2)
- Nehemiah wept when he contemplated how the walls of Jerusalem were broken down (Neh. 1.4).

Tears of compassion

In Romans 12.15, Paul encourages us to 'weep with those who weep' (ESV). We are a family. We choose to go deeper with one another so we have meaningful connections and conversations, and care for one another. We love others all around us with the Father's love.

God intended the Church to be a community of supernatural compassion. We are to be known for our love. Look at these exhortations about loving one another:

'A new command I give you: Love one another. As I have
loved you, so you must love one another. By this everyone
will know that you are my disciples, if you love one another.'
(John 13.34–35)

> Now that you have purified yourselves by obeying the truth
> so that you have sincere love for each other, love one another
> deeply, from the heart.
> (1 Peter 1.22)

> And this is his command: to believe in the name of
> his Son, Jesus Christ, and to love one another as he
> commanded us.
> (1 John 3.23)

We all struggle at times and need to work together and sustain one another's emotional, physical and spiritual health. St Mary's thrives when everyone takes their responsibility to share the load, regardless of how small or large. We are a family, not just a gathering of individuals. Small groups are key to building the culture of discipleship we want to see, helping us connect and be resilient even through difficulties. Lockdown has fragmented us, but we need to lean into unity and commitment to one another.

Our compassion starts with others in church and then flows out into a broken world, to neighbours, colleagues, those in need and any whom God places in our lives to love. Many tears were shed during the pandemic as the losses were very painful. We are called to weep with people suffering whether physically, mentally, emotionally or spiritually. We need to break the stigma around mental health and love people who are loved by God, just as they are. We need to love the unlovely, the elderly, vulnerable and lonely, and people on the edges of society, as well as people who may outwardly seem to be OK but are really struggling inwardly. We are to be marked by love, love, love!

Do we really love people? Do we really love the lost? Are we allowing God to touch our hearts? The preacher J. H. Jowett wrote about being 'baptised in the spirit of suffering compassion'. He said, 'Tearless hearts can never be heralds of The Passion. We must bleed if we would be ministers of the saving blood.'[2] Do we care that people perish? Do we see the poor? Do we love the outsider? Perhaps we are too guarded emotionally from the reality of a fallen, broken, lost humanity? Is that why we are so unmoved?

I feel so conscious of our need to love those who have not yet come to Christ. I remember at university, when I did lots of street evangelism, I used to go out for a walk sometimes and just sit and watch people go by, asking God to increase my love. I did not want to minister out of duty, but out of compassion. We have lost this and need to get back to the tear-saturated gospel. This is the only way to speak about coming judgement and sin or God's grace and unconditional mercy: through loving tears.

Tears of conviction

On the theme of the gospel and loving people, I find it amazing how easy it is to take the cross for granted. How can we be so unmoved by what Jesus did for us, so overfamiliar with and unaffected by God's sacrificial love shown in Jesus' birth, death and resurrection? Our gospel is incredible. It is awesome and I never get tired of hearing about Jesus and his love.

Perhaps the root of conviction of sin is when we see ourselves as we really are, and God as he really is; our hearts are filled with such an awe of God, loathing of our sin and awareness of God's love that we simply run to Christ for mercy and salvation.

In 2014, I spent some time with a small group of people who had lived through and experienced that remarkable outpouring of revival on Lewis. They said there was 'a lot of weeping' over conviction of sin and a concern for others' eternal destiny. Agnes, one of those dear saints who was then in her eighties, described the first night of the revival as people came home from the meeting quietly

---

2   W. Duewel, *Ablaze for God* (Grand Rapids, MI: Zondervan, 1989), pp. 244–5.

weeping under both conviction of sin and a profound revelation of the love of God. She described it as 'holy ground'. 'The presence of the Lord was everywhere.' There was a holy solemnity concerning eternity, a depth of fellowship, an atmosphere of praise and worship. The whole atmosphere was full of God. There was a fear of the Lord and an intimate reverence and nearness to God. There was a concern for the lost people in the community. I long for both a deep conviction of sin and a revelation of God's love to sweep into my community. I am sure there would be a lot of tears as God saturated people with conviction of sin and the revelation of God's love.

I love the description of Robert Bruce, a Scottish preacher in the 1580s. 'He made an earthquake upon his hearers and rarely preached, but to a weeping audience.'[3] Another example of this powerful ministry of conviction comes from a Communion Season in Uig in Scotland. John Macdonald of Ferintosh, who lived in the early eighteenth century,

> preached with the Holy Ghost sent down from heaven. The great congregation were smitten as by a mighty wind and the people were laid prostrate on the earth. There were loud outcries. The precentors [worship leaders] . . . sang, but the congregation was overcome with silence. A minister acting, officiating at that occasion, said that 'when he removed the Communion cloths from the tables, they were as wet with the tears of the communicants as though they had been dipped in water.'[4]

That is conviction of sin, but it always leads to life, to new birth and tremendous blessing. What an amazing picture of revival, that the communion linen was wet with tears of repentance!

---

3 T. Lennie, *Land of Many Revivals: Scotland's extraordinary legacy of Christian revivals over four centuries (1527–1857)* (Fearn: Christian Focus Publications, 2015), p. 44.

4 Lennie, *Land of Many Revivals*, p. 246.

Tears of intercession

I want to weep as I feel very deeply about this moment in our nation. The writer of Psalm 119 said, 'Streams of tears flow from my eyes, for your law is not obeyed' (verse 136). This love for people often finds itself best manifested in prayer. The early Methodist preacher Thomas Collins wrote, 'I went to my lonely retreat among the rocks. I wept much as I besought the Lord to give me souls.'[5] Oswald Smith writes of Thomas Collins:

> He gave himself unto prayer. Woods and lonely wayside places became closets. In such exercise time flew unheeded. He stopped amid the solitary crags to pray, and Heaven so met him there that hours elapsed unconsciously. Strong in the might of such baptisms, he became bold to declare the cross, and willing to bear it.[6]

What an example to those of us who preach today!

We are so keen to try anything and everything, except the ancient path of tears. We have ideas, creativity, blue-sky thinking, initiatives, fresh expressions . . . The list is endless and the outcomes negligible. John George Govan put it simply. He said, 'If one is going to be used of God, one must be a good deal alone.'[7] This is the place of love-saturated intercession. Today, we are keen to do anything to be relevant, but sadly we neglect so much that used to actually work such as the power of surrendered life, waiting on God in prayer, deep fellowship, conviction of sin, the prayer meeting, family worship, preaching the new birth, commitment, sacrifice and, also, weeping and love-filled intercession.

---

5   O. J. Smith, *The Passion for Souls* (Lakeland: The Chaucer Press, 1983), p. 31.

6   Smith, *The Passion for Souls*, p. 31.

7   I. R. Govan, *Spirit of Revival* (Edinburgh: Faith Mission, 1978), p. 34.

I love the Hungry venue at New Wine. I will never forget one day in 2018, seeing over 100 people come to the front weeping, prostrate and praying. A time of prayer and weeping over the missing revival. Bodies just lying on the ground crying to God.

In 1907, Joseph Kemp described the prayer meetings in Charlotte Chapel, Edinburgh, which was experiencing revival. He wrote:

> Did anyone ever see such meetings? They used to begin at 7 o'clock on Sunday mornings, but it was felt to be far too late in the day for the great business that had to be transacted before the Throne of Heavenly Grace. The meetings now begin at 6 o'clock and go on for almost seven days a week, with occasional intervals to attend to business, household duties and bodily sustenance. It is that continuous, persevering, God-honouring weekly campaign of prayer that has moved the mighty hand of God to pour upon this favoured people the blessings of His grace in such abundance, and if you should ever be asked the secret of this church's great spiritual prosperity, you can tell them of the prayer meetings.[8]

The sixteenth-century preacher John Welsh, son-in-law of John Knox, spent hours daily in private prayer. His wife would 'sometimes get up in the middle of the night looking for him, only to find him prostrate in the garden or on the floor of the church, weeping and wrestling in intercession for the souls of his parishioners'. His heart was broken for 'the souls of some 3,000 parishioners and he knew not where many of them stood with the Lord'.[9]

Joel prophesied in Joel 2.17:

---

8   B. H. Edwards, *Revival: A people saturated with God* (Darlington: Evangelical Press, 1990), p. 129.

9   Lennie, *Land of Many Revivals*, p. 49.

Let the priests, who minister before the LORD, weep between the portico and the altar. Let them say, 'Spare your people, LORD. Do not make your inheritance an object of scorn, a byword among the nations. Why should they say among the peoples, "Where is their God?"'

Is it not time yet for Christian leaders to weep over our nation again?

I learned passion in prayer as a teenager from watching other praying people around me who groaned with praying love. Prayer was caught, not taught. I still believe the greatest form of prayer today is not about getting the correct words, but about praying with an aching heart of love. Jesus prayed with loud cries and tears. Hebrews 5.7 says, 'During the days of Jesus' life on earth, he offered up prayers and petitions with fervent cries and tears to the one who could save him from death, and he was heard because of his reverent submission.'

Tears of joy

I hope you have known times when the Lord felt so near that all you could do was kneel and weep before him, filled with a consuming desire for the glory of Jesus. This comes when we encounter God as he is and when that happens, everything comes into eternal perspective. Worship never overcomplicates things. It is all about love!

Jeremiah was a weeping prophet most of the time, but he also proclaimed hope, rebuilding and joy. In Jeremiah 31.7–9, we read:

This is what the LORD says:
'Sing with joy for Jacob;
    shout for the foremost of the nations.
Make your praises heard, and say,

"LORD, save your people,
the remnant of Israel."
See, I will bring them from the land of the north
and gather them from the ends of the earth.
Among them will be the blind and the lame,
expectant mothers and women in labour;
a great throng will return.
They will come with weeping;
they will pray as I bring them back.
I will lead them beside streams of water
on a level path where they will not stumble,
because I am Israel's father,
and Ephraim is my firstborn son.'

This weeping was joyful and filled with worship, thanksgiving and gratitude. These are tears of freedom and gladness. Let me say something that too often gets forgotten. The gospel is a gospel of joy! There is celebration, rejoicing, dancing and blessing in Christ. Sometimes weeping is painful, but there is also an unspeakable joy that can only be expressed in tears. May we be more and more saturated in those joyful tears.

Psalm 126.5 reminds us that, 'Those who sow with tears will reap with songs of joy.' This is one of those amazing paradoxes of God's kingdom:[10]

- We can see unseen things (2 Cor. 4.18)
- We conquer by yielding (Rom. 12.20–21)
- We rest under a yoke (Matt. 11.28–30)
- We become great by becoming little (Matt. 18.4)
- We become wise by becoming foolish (1 Cor. 1.20–21)
- We become free by becoming slaves (Rom. 6.17–22)

---

10 J. Drysdale, *The Price of Revival* (Birkenhead: Emmanuel, 1946), p. 182.

- We possess all things by having nothing (2 Cor. 6.10)
- When we are weak, then we are strong (2 Cor. 12.10)
- We live by dying (John 12.24–25).

Sowing in tears means one day we will reap in joy. That is a promise to hold on to in our weeping, praying, conviction, intercession and evangelism. May our God-saturated love bring forth much fruit and joy.

'Jesus wept' (John 11.35)

Everyone knows the shortest verse in the Bible, but there is something here we really need to hear. Jesus cried. He really wept!

Tears are uncomfortable and can feel awkward. Jesus shows us here that he is not emotionally neutral. This is Jesus' response to death and the pain of grief. Yet it is also his vulnerable way of identifying with all of us as we also live with the tension of pain and faith.

This is such a powerful moment of vulnerability as we see Jesus break down and cry. Apart from the cross itself, this is one of the most vulnerable moments we get with Jesus. Vulnerability can be defined as: 'An openness to being wounded which is motivated by the love of God and is the outcome of a voluntary relinquishment of power to protect oneself from being wounded'.[11] Jesus is opening himself to the pain of the world and he weeps.

It is helpful to take a few moments to reflect on Jesus weeping. Some tears in this world are fake, some are a sign of stress. But here, for Jesus, his tears were utterly genuine and real. Mann and Herrick have reflected on this, saying:

Perhaps it is rather a willingness for things to be seen (for a moment at least) exactly as they are. Perhaps it is a decision,

---

11 V. Herrick and I. Mann, *Jesus Wept* (London: Darton, Longman & Todd, 2000), chap. 5.

a choosing to put aside the mask; to strip off for a time the protective clothing of status and the expectations of others. Perhaps it is a resolve to risk transparency and to choose to follow the way of vulnerability. For somewhere between the tears of strain and the tears of manipulation are the genuine tears (whether they are allowed to fall or not) of the human-ness of those who are called to lead the Christian community.[12]

Let's take off our masks, risk vulnerability, follow the weeping prophet Jeremiah and the weeping Saviour Jesus. Let's allow God's mighty love to so penetrate our hearts that our dry eyes and hard heart are melted and we can weep tears of love, repentance, inter-cession, conviction and also joy! This is all about deep love. God save us from loveless, dry, cold Christianity. Let us weep a fountain of tears!

---

12 Herrick and Mann, *Jesus Wept*, p. 4.

10

'Wells of salvation': *sharing Jesus*

> *With joy you will draw water*
> *from the wells of salvation.*
> (Isaiah 12.3)

Our land needs the gospel more than anything. We need salvation in our desperate times. Isaiah 12.3 prophesies 'wells of salvation'. Our God saves and the gospel is our only real hope. We proclaim and live out the one message that can save humanity.

Sharing Jesus is like gladly drawing refreshing water to quench the spiritual thirst of a dry and parched people. We are on a mission together, a mission that is focused on Jesus. We share the gospel in words and actions. Our core calling is to be an outward-focused Church, helping others come to know Jesus. We exist to bring good news. Everything we receive from him we give away.

How can we best reach our communities? Along with that of every other church, our own mission field is vast. God is calling every one of us to share Jesus. Our focus is on helping people of every age and stage take the next step towards faith in Jesus. Our outreach is best when based on the depth of our relationships and community connections. We need to let down our nets on the other side (John 21.6) and see a big catch of people for Jesus.

The gospel is not a side-issue

What does your church put at the centre? Communion? Worship? Community? Relevance? Fund-raising? Events? Courses? Paul told us the heart of his ministry: 'Christ and him crucified' (1 Cor. 2.2).

For some time now, we have been tragically missing a clear gospel DNA at the heart of the wider Church. The gospel is not a side-issue. It is the heart, the core, the centre of our faith. The gospel is crucial, necessary, imperative and indispensable. We need a proclamation and demonstration of repentance and faith, the new birth and the kingdom of God. The very nature of repentance and faith is to be lived out. It is so important to see people genuinely born again. Eternity is at stake.

Churches which focus on just being more churchy will make no impact on the world around them. How sad, how dry, how inexcusable! This is a huge moment for churches with a gospel heart and mission impulse. Revival is a gospel movement. The theme of revival preaching is always the simple and powerful way of salvation in Christ alone.

There is real joy in sharing Jesus. This is too often a side-issue in today's churches, left to those with a passion for mission. If the gospel is mentioned, we often only share part of the message because we are too embarrassed to highlight the problem of human sin. Often we also neglect to proclaim the gospel of the kingdom, with signs and wonders. Only the full gospel brings full joy. Churches that focus inwards will be disappointed, but churches that focus on the gospel will grow with joy.

Redefining the gospel?

Is the authentic New Testament gospel recognisable in the western Church today? Along with relegating the message, we have often diluted it and even redefined it. A different gospel is not fit for purpose to bring the revival we need. Jesus is far more than an interesting addition to add existential meaning to our self-centred lives. We need to regain an emphasis on conviction of sin, revelation of God's love, repentance and forgiveness through the cross and the coming kingdom of God. Be careful you don't proclaim a different or false gospel; an accommodating, easy-on-the-ear, popular, prosperity, accessory gospel, devoid of truth. Jesus is not just a great extra to life, more like a self-help guru or lifestyle app than a Saviour.

This redefinition has caused a paralysis of confidence as many Christians feel ashamed, uncomfortable, even embarrassed by the genuine gospel. The truth is that the gospel does not accommodate the culture. It is not politically correct and never will be. It is not mainstream. It is not popular and it has a cutting edge.

The issue is with the Church. We don't want to offend people. We don't want to talk about sin, lostness or hell, especially hell. No wonder there is a lack of urgency and a lack of love. We need to be saturated with love and compassion to speak of these things.

Why should anyone become a Christian in the first place? What actually is the gospel? If there is no problem and everyone is actually OK and all are heading for heaven no matter what, then none of these gospel issues need to be mentioned. The problem is we ask people to come to Christ when they don't even realise they are lost. If everyone is going to be fine, and evangelism is not that important, why did Jesus have to die on the cross and rise again?

The gospel is salvation from sin and death through Jesus' death and resurrection. Or, as John Owen called it: the death of death in the death of Christ. The gate of salvation is the way to also experiencing God's kingdom of wholeness and healing power. The gospel answers the problem of our sin, which is incompatible with God's holiness; through the cross, Jesus paid the penalty for our sin. He took our sin and sorrow. He died for us, in our place, and rose again, defeating death and hell. Jesus is Saviour from sin and Lord of all. He brings us from death to life and darkness to light. The way of salvation has always been, and ever will be, to repent and believe in Jesus.

This simple, powerful and unchanged gospel is at the heart of every genuine revival. Churches don't change nations; the gospel does. We are called to plant the gospel, not just churches. The gospel is unchained, powerful and has the power to change our nation. The contemporary Church has too easily forgotten the power of the full gospel. Perhaps we now need to return to the simplicity of living out the gospel message to see revival come and our churches adding people daily to those being saved.

Could part of the way to revival be living out and proclaiming the whole gospel? This was what burned in the hearts of John Wesley, George Whitefield and William Booth. Renewal and revival were birthed through the gospel. Our entire Christian inheritance and ongoing renewal have come not through the Church as an institution, but through the Church as birthed by the gospel.

The gospel is the lifeblood of revival

Revivals are always marked by large numbers of conversions to Christ. This is what changes communities and nations; not events, programmes, courses and best efforts in evangelism. These have their place, but we need more than mere methods to meet the needs of today. We need community-changing conversions. We need hundreds, thousands and, indeed, millions to turn to follow Jesus Christ if we are to see real change and society transformed.

It is vital to remember that conversion to Christ is thoroughly biblical:

Repent, then, and turn to God, so that your sins may be wiped out, that times of refreshing may come from the Lord.
(Acts 3.19)

The King James Bible puts it this way:

Repent ye therefore, and be converted, that your sins may be blotted out, when the times of refreshing shall come from the presence of the Lord.

142

Here we see the link between repentance, conversation, revival and transformation. This was the New Testament model for changing nations. It was a gospel plan. Not big budget, not seeker sensitive, not community organising – just gospel life and power experienced, lived, proclaimed and shared. What is stopping us from adopting this dynamic gospel core? We applaud all things novel, but seem to dismiss the very passion and essential ingredient needed: the gospel.

Is the gospel at the very core of our churches? Romans 1.16 reminds us the gospel is the power of God that brings salvation to all who believe:

> For I am not ashamed of the gospel, because it is the power of God that brings salvation to everyone who believes: first to the Jew, then to the Gentile.

What do we need today?

1 *We need a core gospel conviction.* The gospel of the kingdom is what changes us. This is where we find hope, salvation, forgiveness, redemption, reconciliation and healing. The cross is at the centre and we depend on the power of the Spirit. Our confidence in the gospel is paramount. There is power when we fully embrace and joyfully and unashamedly share the gospel.

2 *We need an urgency and passion for people in spiritual need.* What is the value of a soul? I wonder whether five minutes into eternity we will wish we could have our time over again because we can see the inestimable value of every human life from an eternal perspective. The Bible reminds us there is an eternal destiny awaiting all people (Rev. 20.11–12). In Romans 9, Paul wished himself accursed for the sake of saving others. There is an urgency. Five minutes into eternity will be too late for regrets.

3 *We need to pray for people who are lost without Jesus.* According to Acts 1, we need prayer to precede our witness. Prayer for people to be saved is the most important prayer burden. This is the greatest need and our highest prayer request. People who don't know Jesus as Saviour and Lord won't spend the weekend in heaven or hell. It is for eternity. Really loving people means pointing them from hell to heaven!

Let's put our best energy into evangelism and saving souls. In this gospel-moment after the pandemic, and with extraordinarily complex global problems, now is the time to get back to soul-winning love and confidence in the gospel that works.

Let me challenge you: when did you last share the whole gospel with anyone? Have you ever led another person to Christ? Are you focused on planting the gospel of the kingdom?

I feel truly alive when sharing Jesus with others. There is such a thrill in pointing thirsty souls to the life-giving water of Jesus. The gospel is pure and refreshing living water. It isn't just a gate to heaven, it is the gospel of the King's kingdom, which means there is also healing, reconciliation, wholeness and peace in this life. Everyone needs the 'well of salvation'. Everyone needs to be rescued by Jesus and to belong to Jesus.

When I heard God call me into ministry, it was through Acts 26.16–18:

'Now get up and stand on your feet. I have appeared to you
to appoint you as a servant and as a witness of what you
have seen and will see of me. I will rescue you from your
own people and from the Gentiles. I am sending you to
them to open their eyes and turn them from darkness to
light, and from the power of Satan to God, so that they may
receive forgiveness of sins and a place among those who are
sanctified by faith in me.'

I know this word came to Paul at his own dramatic conversion, but when I read those words sitting on a bench outside my secondary school, I knew somehow that God was speaking to me too. I heard the call to stand up, to become a servant and witness of the gospel. I had been saved; now I was being sent. I wanted to help open people's eyes to Jesus. To turn people from darkness to light, from the devil to Jesus, so that they might experience forgiveness and salvation, and also that they might belong to Jesus for ever as his holy people. I caught that vision for mission and evangelism, for sharing Jesus. I want everyone to catch this missionary vision.

Everyone equipped to share Jesus and plant the gospel

Not only is it a missionary vision; it is a multiplying vision. Revival multiplies and intensifies mission. Many people come to faith in a clear way. Perhaps we need fewer events and more equipping, so we can multiply more and more disciples and churches.

I love the flow of Luke 9—10, which is an unfolding story of Jesus taking risks, empowering others and sending people on mission together. This is a river of gospel power moving through ordinary people, multiplying and transforming lives.

Let's start at Luke 9.1–6, as Jesus sends out the Twelve:

When Jesus had called the Twelve together, he gave them power and authority to drive out all demons and to cure diseases, and he sent them out to proclaim the kingdom of God and to heal the sick. He told them: 'Take nothing for the journey – no staff, no bag, no bread, no money, no extra shirt. Whatever house you enter, stay there until you leave that town. If people do not welcome you, leave their town and shake the dust off your feet as a testimony against them.' So they set out and went from village to village, proclaiming the good news and healing people everywhere.

What a mission! Jesus had a core conviction of the gospel of the kingdom. He wanted everyone to experience whole salvation in body, mind and soul. There was both proclamation of the good news and demonstration of the Spirit's power. The disciples were sent out in dependency and unity. They were sent out with power! Power to heal and also to live by faith, and to do it together in small teams. They were sent out knowing they would not be popular or welcome everywhere, but it worked and they started seeing people healed everywhere!

It doesn't end there. Sharing Jesus is more than that. Jesus went on in Luke 9 to feed 5,000 men, plus their families. The story moves on as Peter declares Jesus is the Messiah and then Jesus predicts his death in Luke 9.22:

> Then he said to them all: 'Whoever wants to be my disciple
> must deny themselves and take up their cross daily and
> follow me. For whoever wants to save their life will lose it,
> but whoever loses their life for me will save it.'
> (Luke 9.23–24)

We get the whole gospel in Luke. There is a life-side of healing and salvation, but also a death-side of dying to self and living out the cost of following Jesus. We lose our own lives when we belong to Jesus. In doing so we find the life that is really life!

Still in Luke 9, we move into the transfiguration, Jesus heals a demon-possessed boy and then for a second time predicts his death. In Luke 9.46–50, we continue the gospel stream:

> An argument started among the disciples as to which of
> them would be the greatest. Jesus, knowing their thoughts,

took a little child and had him stand beside him. Then he said to them, 'Whoever welcomes this little child in my name welcomes me; and whoever welcomes me welcomes the one who sent me. For it is the one who is least among you all who is the greatest.' 'Master,' said John, 'we saw someone driving out demons in your name and we tried to stop him, because he is not one of us.' 'Do not stop him,' Jesus said, 'for whoever is not against you is for you.'

Jesus says the greatest in his kingdom are the least in our way of thinking. We need to receive the gospel like little children. We need to dive in by faith!

After a disappointing episode in Luke 9.51–56, where the disciples had suggested calling down fire on Samaritans because they were unwelcoming, Jesus rebuked them. At this point, Jesus would have been forgiven for cancelling the ministry school he had recently started. He had taken a risk and it seemed to have back-fired. The disciples kept messing up in ministry. What would you do?

Luke 9 ends up reflecting on the cost of following Jesus:

As they were walking along the road, a man said to him, 'I will follow you wherever you go.' Jesus replied, 'Foxes have dens and birds have nests, but the Son of Man has no place to lay his head.' He said to another man, 'Follow me.' But he replied, 'Lord, first let me go and bury my father.' Jesus said to him, 'Let the dead bury their own dead, but you go and proclaim the kingdom of God.' Still another said, 'I will follow you, Lord; but first let me go back and say goodbye to my family.' Jesus replied, 'No one who puts a hand to the plough and looks back is fit for service in the kingdom of God.'
(Luke 9.57–62)

Can we see in these verses just how highly Jesus values mission? No matter what, we are to proclaim the kingdom of God, to share Jesus. Is that how we see things?

Amazingly, after all that, in Luke 10.1, Jesus ups the ante again and this time sends out 72 people!

> After this the Lord appointed seventy-two others and sent them two by two ahead of him to every town and place where he was about to go. He told them, 'The harvest is plentiful, but the workers are few. Ask the Lord of the harvest, therefore, to send out workers into his harvest field. Go! I am sending you out like lambs among wolves. Do not take a purse or bag or sandals; and do not greet anyone on the road. When you enter a house, first say, "Peace to this house."'
> (Luke 10.1–5)

The harvest is plentiful. The world needs Jesus. But the workers are few!

> The seventy-two returned with joy and said, 'Lord, even the demons submit to us in your name.' He replied, 'I saw Satan fall like lightning from heaven. I have given you authority to trample on snakes and scorpions and to overcome all the power of the enemy; nothing will harm you. However, do not rejoice that the spirits submit to you, but rejoice that your names are written in heaven.'
> (Luke 10.17–20)

Here we have a real mission going on where the power of God is moving, miracles are happening, yet the most important thing to Jesus is that the missionaries' names are written in heaven; they are born again! This is the gospel of the kingdom! A full, free, powerful and life-changing gospel, which is badly needed again today in our world.

The full gospel calls for everyone to engage, to step into whatever part they can play in God's mission to multiply his kingdom through us.

- Could you do something new that will reach people with the gospel?
- How might you do something to increase your confidence in sharing Jesus?
- Why not increase your regular giving to the mission of the Church?
- Do you need to step down from one area of ministry and take up a new one?

Don't we want to move beyond being resource churches to being revival churches? What are we multiplying? The gospel!

This joyful drawing of water from the well of salvation is a vital element in seeking revival. We long to see individuals, hundreds, thousands and even millions, trust in Christ for whole salvation. May the river of gospel life and kingdom life flow in our homes, communities and nations. Open up the wells of salvation in this land!

If we want to learn, grow and move in being saturated with God, let's get drenched in his gospel wells every day.

11

'There is a river': encountering God

There is a river whose streams make glad the city of God,
the holy place where the Most High dwells.
(Psalm 46.4)

A mark of true revival is the overwhelming and irresistible presence of God coming down in a community, town or region. In a community saturated with God, people encounter God's glory; they can never be the same again. In revival, people encounter God everywhere. This also calls us to cultivate a deeper encounter with God in our everyday lives.

There must be more than this; more than we currently experience with whole communities still largely untouched by God's kingdom. There is much more of God to encounter, and not only in church or on Sundays. God wants us to experience and encounter him all the time.

There is a river of life-changing encounter that Jesus invites us into. Jesus died and rose again so we could enter the streams of God's intimate presence. Who will swim in the river of God today? Who will go deeper? Recently in church, I had a prophetic picture of us standing in a puddle, when there was a rushing river available. This river is the place of an authentic and fruitful encounter with God. Jesus wants us to really know him. This is what Paul was crying out for in Philippians 3.10: 'I want to know Christ – yes, to know the power of his resurrection and participation in his sufferings, becoming like him in his death . . .'

We were made for deep relationship with God; intimacy with God through time in prayer, the Bible, worship and listening to his voice. From this place of encounter, we depend on the Holy Spirit in daily life. This is a time to slow down to meet God. The world is waiting for people who really know their God! There are no short-cuts, just ancient paths to intimacy.

Deeper than ever before

The good news is that 'there is a river' of God, yet sadly there are few who seem to make their home there. There are few who seem to really go deep in God. I believe we need to put aside our dehy-drated and insufficient, limited knowledge of God, and humbly begin to go deeper, and to get further into the river than we have ever been before. Who will go there? Where are the saturated ones? Where are the people who have left puddles behind and are fully submerged in the river of God?

This image of the river of God is from Ezekiel 47.1–12:

I saw water coming out from under the threshold of the temple towards the east (for the temple faced east). The water was coming down from under the south side of the temple, south of the altar. He then brought me out through the north gate and led me round the outside to the outer gate facing east, and the water was trickling from the south side. As the man went eastward with a measuring line in his hand, he measured off a thousand cubits and then led me through water that was ankle-deep. He measured off another thousand cubits and led me through water that was knee-deep. He measured off another thousand and led me through water that was up to the waist. He measured off another thousand, but now it was a river that I could not cross, because the water had risen and was deep enough to swim in – a river that no one could cross. He asked me, 'Son of man, do you see this?' Then he led me back to the bank of the river. When I arrived there, I saw a great number of trees on each side of the river. He said to me, 'This water flows towards the eastern region and goes down into the Arabah, where it enters the Dead Sea. When it empties into the sea, the salty water there becomes fresh. Swarms of living creatures will live wherever the river flows. There will be large numbers of fish, because this water flows there and makes the salt water fresh; so where the river flows everything will live. Fishermen will stand along the shore; from En Gedi to En Eglaim there will be places for spreading nets. The fish will be of many kinds – like the fish of the Mediterranean Sea. But the swamps and marshes will not become fresh; they will be left for salt. Fruit trees of all kinds will grow on both banks of the river. Their leaves will not wither, nor will their fruit fail. Every month they will bear fruit, because the water from the sanctuary flows to them. Their fruit will serve for food and their leaves for healing.'

This prophetic picture of the river is packed with truth we desperately need in our time. In the river we see various depths of encounter with God that we can choose to experience. We can go as deep in God as we really want to. The thirstier we are, the deeper we go. The more we want God to move, the more he will move.

There is a choice here about the level of encounter you and I are going to settle with. Most of us choose a comfortable level. Letting the Spirit move so much, and no further. Many of us are content for our experience of the river of God to be ankle-, knee- or even waist-deep; but not yet swimming. God wants us to go deeper still and to swim, not just paddle, in his presence.

This scripture paints a beautiful picture of the coming of the Holy Spirit bringing new life and healing. The river of God is a powerful image of revival and refreshing. The river speaks of the presence of God flowing into and also out from churches and communities. What a difference encountering God makes!

The river flows into the Dead Sea where it causes the salt water to become fresh. That is impossible! But, nothing is impossible with God! The truth is that 'where the river flows everything will live' (verse 9). Fish will be teeming there and healing trees will grow on the riverbanks. What a vibrant picture of abundant life.

This is a mighty river of redemption, healing, fellowship, anointing, conviction and worship. It is an inflow of the kingdom of God into communities. It is something supernatural, powerful, God-ordained and totally different to programme-led church. How might we let the river flow in our churches and into our communities?

We get another glimpse of this awesome river of God in Revelation 22.1–5:

> Then the angel showed me the river of the water of life, as clear as crystal, flowing from the throne of God and of the Lamb down the middle of the great street of the city. On each side of the river stood the tree of life, bearing twelve crops of fruit, yielding its fruit every month. And the leaves of the tree are for the healing of the nations. No longer will there be any curse. The throne of God and of the Lamb will be in the city, and his servants will serve him. They will see his face, and his name will be on their foreheads. There will be no more night. They will not need the light of a lamp or the light of the sun, for the Lord God will give them light. And they will reign for ever and ever.

This river of God's awesome presence is about the redemption of all creation and Jesus making everything new when he comes again and we see a new heaven and earth. We will see this river flow with tremendous healing power. There is just something glorious, eternal and hopeful about this heavenly river of God. We look forward to this day coming.

The river of God also reminds me that this is not a man-made river. It is not about us, by us or from us in our humanity. This is the river *of God*. God is the Saviour, Healer, Redeemer, Reviver, Saturator!

We see this illustrated powerfully again by the parting of sea waters in Exodus 14.10–16:

> As Pharaoh approached, the Israelites looked up, and there were the Egyptians, marching after them. They were terrified and cried out to the LORD. They said to Moses, 'Was it because there were no graves in Egypt that you brought us to the desert to die? What have you done to us by bringing us out of Egypt? Didn't we say to you in Egypt, "Leave us alone; let us serve the Egyptians"? It would have been better for us to serve the Egyptians than to die in the desert!' Moses answered the people, 'Do not be afraid. Stand firm and you will see the deliverance the LORD will bring you today. The Egyptians you see today you will never see again. The LORD will fight for you; you need only to be still.' Then the LORD said to Moses, 'Why are you crying out to me? Tell the Israelites to move on. Raise your staff and stretch out your hand over the sea to divide the water so that the Israelites can go through the sea on dry ground.'

Our God is the God of miracles, the God of deliverance. He is a nation-changing God. He fights for us. He moves and everything changes. This is 100 per cent God at work. He used Moses, but Moses had no power over the sea water. God's Spirit worked the miracle as Moses obeyed him. Here is the lesson for us. Revival is God at work! It is God who convicts of sin. It is God who saves.

It is God who heals. It is God who brings freedom. It is God who builds the Church. It is God who reveals his love. This means there is always hope that he will break through and do the impossible. Looking at the incredible river of God in Scripture, when God is on the move and his river is flowing, nothing is impossible.

There must be more

Knowing that this river of God can flow into our towns and villages must make a difference to how we live, pray, worship and believe. You would think so! Yet, there is a whole realm of encounter that many Christians don't seem aware of, much less hungry for.

Let me share a prophetic picture a member of our church shared with me which they felt could be relevant to the whole Church:

I felt God was grieving at the state of the bride, that we are not yet fit and prepared. I sensed there was a fear of the Holy Spirit in the church that was showing itself as a bride wanting to control the bridegroom, a fear of surrendering to him. I felt Jesus was saying he wants a bride that trusts him, that is yielded to him. A bride that loves him deeply, who seeks to know what he is thinking, what pleases him, who has insight into what he's doing. A bride that knows how he feels about her; who has confidence in his love for her. Jesus doesn't want a bride who is frightened of surrendering or who wants to control or limit him. He doesn't want a bride that's coerced, an 'arranged' marriage or a bride that just wants him for his power and to spend his wealth. We are all beloved children of God but I feel there is a fresh invitation from God to go deeper, to walk in greater intimacy, to know a new level of courage, power and love – to become the bride. So that he can bring the transformation that's needed in our lives, in the lives of our families and communities and in the wider world.

There is so much more, but sadly, we are not ready! We are too fearful, too withdrawn, too selfish and unyielded. Do you recognise your church in this prophetic picture? As Natasha Crain put it, 'Christians are often living more as an *extension* of the secular world today, than a distinct light *to* it.'[1] All the while, God has prepared a river of his presence for us, but we sadly choose our puddles!

God's river is a flood of rich relationship, intimate knowledge and joyful trembling in his presence, with Jesus at the centre. This is more than goose bumps for our favourite worship song or Bible verse. God's presence is altogether deeper, more real and radiant.

Do we really know and encounter God? Not just having heard from someone about him, but knowing him personally. Knowing God personally is such a basic part of being a Christian, yet it doesn't seem that many people live as though they actually know the God revealed in the Bible.

Where are the saturated, deep, river-swimming Christians? People with substance in their relationship with God, who know how to feed themselves spiritually and also have learned how to abide in the deep waters of God.

How do you describe knowing God? What does knowing God mean to you? Do we take the time to ever really meditate on this, much less practise the reality? In one of those recordings of Duncan Campbell I listened to as a teenager, I always remember him telling the story of a group of young people who had huge enthusiasm and passion when all meeting together for worship. While praying for them one of Duncan Campbell's friends used a steam train analogy and prayed that their enthusiasm would be like steam which would 'go to the piston', not 'out through the whistle'. How much of our spiritual passion just goes out through the whistle, not into the piston?

---

1 N. Crain, *Faithfully Different: Regaining biblical clarity in a secular culture* (Eugene, OR: Harvest House, 2022), p. 17.

I have always wanted to get to know that presence of God in my own life. I think of this as a nearness, company and closeness with God. Those I have met who know God intimately seem to live from that encounter. They have an intimacy, connection, experience and contact with God which I long to also experience more and more. I have always believed the simple truth that encountering God changes everything. I honestly believe that, but I still find myself sometimes pulling back and feeling unworthy to enter his presence, because to encounter God is to stand on holy ground. For me, it all springs from encountering a depth of God's love and his Father's heart. I have never known another love like his.

As I reflect on my own encounters over the years, I feel drawn out after God again. He fully satisfies, yet we always want more of him. My encounters with God seem both ordinary and extraordinary. He speaks to me and meets me by his grace in the everyday things of life, yet when he moves, speaks or reveals his presence it is continually life-changing.

Getting soaked in God

People often ask me what I really mean by encountering God. I think they expect me to talk about the supernatural, spectacular or extraordinary. The tough thing is that most of us don't have those kinds of experiences very often, if at all. I have had some encounters like that, but honestly, they are few and far between. Most of the time, I believe in encountering God in everyday, faithful, obedient, sacrificial, sometimes uncomfortable discipleship. It isn't very sensational, but it is absolutely saturating. I am talking about prayer, Bible reading, meditation on the Word, prophecy, worship, conviction, mission, passionate prayer meetings, anointed preaching of the gospel, family worship, sacrificial serving, full surrender and obedience, humbling ourselves, commitment to the church body, kingdom justice and social action, repentance, confession, restitution and reconciliation. We can encounter God in all this and more.

Let the Bible shape our expectation of his presence, as well as our whole world-view. Can I encourage us all to become engaged Bible readers and also to take time to pray alone? The more we get back to these ancient and simple paths, the nearer we will be to revival.

So much effort goes into re-organising, re-imagining and re-packaging ministry. What we need is more of God!

Let's consider some biblical soaking images about seeking God's powerful presence. In Hosea 10.12, we find the prophet waiting and crying out, '[I]t is time to seek the LORD, until he comes and showers his righteousness on you.' What a beautiful image of being saturated in righteousness. Seeking God releases that rain of righteousness into your family and community. The way to soak is to seek.

Look at what happened in Ezekiel 1.28. He encountered God:

> like the appearance of a rainbow in the clouds on a rainy day,
> so was the radiance around him. This was the appearance of
> the likeness of the glory of the LORD. When I saw it, I fell face
> down, and I heard the voice of one speaking.

Ezekiel was not living from the borrowed encounters of knowing God second-hand. We need to meet God ourselves. His reaction was to fall face down. This was a dramatic encounter, but it soaked him so much that his life changed and he became a prophet. Not an easy calling. Much of the trouble Ezekiel went on to suffer would have been met by the resource from his meeting with God.

Consider also Isaiah's invitation in Isaiah 55.1:

> 'Come, all you who are thirsty,
>   come to the waters;

and you who have no money,
  come, buy and eat!
Come, buy wine and milk
  without money and without cost.'

There is the simple call to the thirsty to 'come'. A profound need is met by an abundant supply. Our poverty is met by grace. Our helplessness is met by God's empowering presence. Our weakness is met by his provision. The price has been fully paid by Jesus, the Suffering Servant (Isa. 53). All paid for! We simply come to Christ. This theme is picked up again in Revelation 21.6: 'He said to me: "It is done. I am the Alpha and the Omega, the Beginning and the End. To the thirsty I will give water without cost from the spring of the water of life."' Then again in Revelation 22.17: 'The Spirit and the bride say, "Come!" And let the one who hears say, "Come!" Let the one who is thirsty come; and let the one who wishes take the free gift of the water of life.'

The heart of encounter is simply in seeking God and coming to Christ. Not on our merits, as everything has been paid for by his precious blood. God's presence is absolutely free to us, but costly to him. We need a revelation of Jesus, the power of his resurrection and fellowship of his suffering (Phil. 3.10). Hope is not returning to 'normal', but going deeper than ever before into the river.

12

'A well-watered garden': *living for the kingdom*

'Is not this the kind of fasting I have chosen:
to loose the chains of injustice
    and untie the cords of the yoke,
to set the oppressed free
    and break every yoke?
Is it not to share your food with the hungry
    and to provide the poor wanderer with shelter –
when you see the naked, to clothe them,
    and not to turn away from your own flesh and blood?
Then your light will break forth like the dawn,
    and your healing will quickly appear;
then your righteousness will go before you,
    and the glory of the LORD *will be your rear guard.*
Then you will call, and the LORD *will answer;*
    you will cry for help, and he will say: here am I.

'If you do away with the yoke of oppression,
    with the pointing finger and malicious talk,
and if you spend yourselves on behalf of the hungry
    and satisfy the needs of the oppressed,
then your light will rise in the darkness,
    and your night will become like the noonday.
The LORD *will guide you always;*
    he will satisfy your needs in a sun-scorched land
    and will strengthen your frame.

You will be like a well-watered garden,
  like a spring whose waters never fail.
Your people will rebuild the ancient ruins
  and will raise up the age-old foundations;
you will be called Repairer of Broken Walls,
  Restorer of Streets with Dwellings.'
(Isaiah 58.6–12)

Every revival movement is also a prominent movement advocating biblical justice and restoration. Isaiah 58 promises we will be like a 'well-watered garden' when we get justice issues right in a way worthy of God's kingdom. How wonderful to be a 'spring whose waters never fail' – what a promise and picture of God's kingdom in saturated renewal.

If we want to experience revival, we must learn to be shaped and formed into well-watered gardens of justice and peace. If we want to promote and experience revival, we must learn the ways of loving our local and global neighbour better, and making it part of everyday life.

People with a heart for kingdom restoration and justice care about ending modern slavery, about mental well-being, creation care and seeing people based on their character, not skin colour. God's justice cares about looking after the poorest and most vulnerable in life. He is the God who sees the weakest and those on the fringes of life, and he goes to them. People with God's heart for living for the kingdom see our broken society racked by sin and cry out for active holiness and meaningful repentance that touch the reality of how we live and the impact we all have today on our local and global neighbour and our entire planet.

God overflows with a passion for setting people free from bondages, strongholds and patterns of sin. Biblical justice, mercy and social action are an essential part of this. This is what we mean by transforming society in the power of the Spirit. This was true of the early Salvation Army, and many other mission movements that were also revival movements. Revival and social action were inseparable for the Methodist Revival in the eighteenth century. Revival always fuels biblical justice.

To be saturated with God is to be marinated in mercy and compassion. This is good news for the poor. We put God first in everything and our lives increasingly reflect God's kingdom. This means growing in Spirit-filled discipleship, mission, social justice, spiritual gifts, healing and freedom. We live the truth that Jesus is Lord. We are 'all in' for the kingdom.

So much of our current dryness is due to our first and foremost meeting our own needs. Our unrestricted greed and selfishness have blurred our spiritual vision. So much so, many in our churches today can't even see the problem. We protest our innocence in vain. We have become incredibly short-sighted and every time we egoistically demote God's attribute of fierce justice to a second-class part of his nature, we expose our own foolishness.

The truth is that living for God's kingdom as a follower of Jesus is not about satisfying our own needs and wants first. This idol of false comfort needs to fall. Let's call it by its real name: greed! It is such a thick darkness in our land. Exposing greed in our culture is hard. This is often when we feel guarded and defensive. Maybe we need to give God our full attention and allow him to convict us of our greed? I have found in my own journey with this that the more I try to excuse my own greed, the less I allow myself to really feel the pain of injustice.

Who is there who shares God's heart of compassion? We are preoccupied with our own sense of overwhelm; we might be missing God's burning heart. Have we really seen the compassion of our Father in heaven? Have we allowed his heart to break our hearts?

Learning to live justly

I am sorry to say that, for years, I undervalued God's heart for justice. My gospel was about seeing souls saved, not yet so much about seeing society transformed in the power of the Spirit. The gospel does open the gate to heaven and eternal life, but it is also good news for our bodies and minds in this life. Now I long to live out more a full gospel of salvation by faith, through grace, in Christ, who calls us to love God and our neighbour as ourselves.

The Bible is so full of this kind of everyday and ordinary, yet also transformational, kingdom living. We are commanded to be just and live justly. Let's look at a few of the scriptures:

> Speak up for those who cannot speak for themselves,
>   for the rights of all who are destitute.
> Speak up and judge fairly;
>   defend the rights of the poor and needy.
> (Proverbs 31.8–9)

> Learn to do right; seek justice.
>   Defend the oppressed.
> Take up the cause of the fatherless;
>   plead the case of the widow.
> (Isaiah 1.17)

> This is what the LORD says: do what is just and right.
> Rescue from the hand of the oppressor the one who has
> been robbed. Do no wrong or violence to the foreigner, the
> fatherless or the widow, and do not shed innocent blood in
> this place.
> (Jeremiah 22.3)

Could God make it any clearer? It is so sad that when it comes to this social holiness, this kingdom living, the Church is currently missing its prophetic voice and has become an echo. We are polite, nice and unwilling to offend, yet ignore the tides of sin and tsunamis of brokenness and pain in our communities.

So how can we repent and learn to live differently? What might living justly look like? I want to be a 'well-watered garden'. I want to be saturated with God, and part of that is learning this way of restoration and God's heart for living justice.

Much as I love great Christian organisations doing this such as Tearfund, International Justice Mission, Every Life and others, I think the best way to learn this life is to see it lived out by passionate followers of Jesus.

I have learned so much from my remarkable wife Caroline. God has given her a beautiful gift of a heart for justice and integrity. Caroline thinks about these things all the time. She really considers how she lives much more than I do. Her life has been such a gift to me as I see her work out how to live for God's kingdom in modern Britain. Seeking simplicity, seeking to reduce our harmful impact on the planet, seeking to reduce our food waste as an act of gospel love and life, seeking to serve people the world simply forgets and devalues.

Caroline leads Living Hope, our community mission in our local church family in St Mary's Loughton. Her lifestyle is prophetic without trying to be. She is not trying to make a statement, but just seeks to love people well, to share Jesus and to find a lifestyle of thoughtful integrity as a follower of Jesus. Every decision we make can lead to an impact on others that may be unjust. So loving Jesus means taking care to consider our impact on others.

I have loved some of the ordinary ways we have explored living justly at home. We have done things like not buying anything brand-new for a whole year, or finding 2,000 items in our home to give away or raising funds for Tearfund by setting a stair-climbing challenge to climb the equivalent of Mount Everest, while raising funds for the world's poorest people. These are things we can learn, grow in, get our children involved with, and share with others. This is living for the kingdom and completely integral to a God-saturated life.

Caroline's life of seeking integrity, justice and compassion lived out in ordinary ways always really challenges me. I would not normally think too hard about where I shop, whom it might impact or what might happen to a particular piece of plastic after it has been thrown away. I have seen God use Caroline's heart powerfully on an issue such as food waste, so much so that various projects on that issue she has established have, over time, fed thousands of people in need. Small acts of justice are multiplied into feeding thousands! Sound familiar?

Living for the kingdom is not about making grand gestures or virtue-signalling; it is about our daily priorities, choices and decisions leaning into God's justice. Daily and unglamorous decisions that think of others and serving, not myself and getting!

Everyday choices in pursuit of ordinary and more just ways of living cover so many issues. God is challenging our complacency and self-reliance and the idolatry of comfort and entitlement. As we face the reality of greed and poverty in today's world, we see injustice everywhere. We need to promote God's justice in a world facing climate change and in communities that have already been devastated by human self-indulgence. Our world faces other huge issues such as the stigma around mental health issues, which needs to be broken. God's justice calls us to real love and compassion. Other real issues people face include hot potatoes such as abortion, sexuality and marriage, and racism. These issues have long divided people, but the gospel of grace transforms people. God is just and we can learn his just ways. What biblical justice issues are you willing to give your life to changing? Here are a few suggestions:

- Local and global poverty, hunger and homelessness
- Injustice such as sex trafficking and exploitation
- People caught in cycles of hopelessness or the stigma of mental health struggles
- Orphans without a home or those who are lonely; going unloved

- Creation being destroyed by man-made greed
- Prisoners abandoned and left without hope or care.

All of us can choose kingdom justice in the power of the Spirit and learn to make a difference.

Learning to love mercy

Kingdom living like a 'well-watered garden' embraces every opportunity for mercy. We are so amazed by the mercy we ourselves have received that it is only right to share it with others. Isn't grace astounding!

Jesus modelled this all the time and taught us clearly to be merciful, just as God the Father is merciful (Luke 6.36). Look what Jesus teaches in Matthew 10.42: 'And if anyone gives even a cup of cold water to one of these little ones who is my disciple, truly I tell you, that person will certainly not lose their reward.' Even small doses of mercy matter. It is about loving the people in front of you and seeing others from God's perspective.

Learning mercy might look like taking time to get to know someone and not rejecting them even though we know their faults. Mercy gives time and care to others. This is powerful within a wider culture that promotes suspicion, offence, fear and unforgiveness and punishment. The amazing thing about mercy is that it brings a miraculous release of forgiveness and finds out how God sees people. Mercy is not a franchise ministry or programme. It is giving, serving, sharing, praying, encouraging and participating.

When I think of learning mercy, I think of sharing community meals in our church with many from the church family and many from the community who are not yet in church. I think of our food bank caring for people week after week. I reflect on caring for people we would otherwise overlook. I consider our amazing experience of having a Ukrainian family live with us, as they were unable to go home due to war. God is teaching us to be merciful. Our home can be a house of miracles.

Revival means more of God's kingdom than we have ever seen before. It means a flowing river of justice, peace, wholeness, welcome, creation care, miracles, inner and emotional healing, deeper relationships and care, hospitality and fellowship, generosity, forgiveness, physical healing, gifts of the Spirit, love and unity, social holiness and kingdom economics. I want to see a revival that touches every part of my community. Not just the nice parts, but every part. God-saturated communities will be turned the right way up! Isn't this what the world is really waiting for?

Learning to walk humbly

Our nation will not be changed through services, but through servants. In John 13.5, we read, 'After that, he poured water into a basin and began to wash his disciples' feet, drying them with the towel that was wrapped round him.' Here is a washing with water that is all about humility. Have you allowed Jesus to wash your feet?

Are we willing to walk humbly as we live for Jesus? We need to let Jesus wash us; to let go of pride, our self-importance and our way of doing things. The Church today needs an old-school and deep-rooted prophetic type of leader, pastor, preacher and intercessor. We need teachable, humble, soft-hearted people today. People willing to pick up a servant towel and wash others' dirty feet, even when it isn't really their job in the first place!

Our God is the God of humility, reconciliation, forgiveness and peace. He is the answer to the injustice, wickedness, division, bitterness, guilt and anxiety in our world. Biblical justice is not the same as secular social justice; it is based on grace, not ideology. We are living in a time when issues of justice are rightly at the forefront. May the Church not be reticent to seek justice. But, we must not allow ideology to lead us. The gospel is more than enough!

167

I am inviting you to join in a journey and adventure of the kingdom in love. To unlearn old habits and thinking and discover God's ways of living out the gospel as Jesus lived and taught it. We long to know more of God and his great love!

Kingdom justice is a love story

This really is all about experiencing and relying on God's love. Jesus calls us his bride, not converts (Eph. 5.25–27; Rev. 19.7–9). As 1 John 4.16 reminds us, 'And so we know and rely on the love God has for us. God is love.'

The story of salvation is a love story. Jesus compares his kingdom to a wedding feast (Matt. 22.2)! It is a love story between God and his people. Our inbuilt longing for love is part of the image of our heavenly Father God. God wants us to know him and love him personally, passionately and intimately.

Living for the kingdom comes from deep relationship with Jesus. Perhaps we are too scared to have a deeper relationship because it will mean some kingdom changes?

There is a God-encounter at the heart of biblical justice. We are invited to experience his radical love and know him personally. Now is the time to be broken and bend our will and surrender to his love; to stop striving and yield ourselves.

Perhaps now would be a good moment to reflect on a time when you were deeply moved by God's love, either for yourself or for others. What happened? How did you respond? What effect has it had? What type of encounter was it?

- *A love encounter* – when you have a revelation of God's amazing love for you
- *A holiness encounter* – when you are cleansed from sin and filled with the Spirit

- *A truth encounter* – when God shows you a truth that has a big impact on your life
- *A power encounter* – when you prayed for someone to be healed
- *A justice encounter* – when you helped care for someone in need.

Are you still living in the experience of that encounter?

Love has to look like something. Justice is about living with a passion for Jesus that means we act very practically. We learn to be just, merciful and humble because of loving Jesus. If we are willing to become servants we will discover true justice, compassion, mercy and humility. Only people who humble themselves can be saturated. Water flows to the lowest places of learning justice, servanthood, mercy, teachability and humility. Such a life is well watered, a never-failing spring.

13

'I will pour out my Spirit on all people': *everyone overflowing*

'And afterwards,
*   I will pour out my Spirit on all people.*
Your sons and daughters will prophesy,
*   your old men will dream dreams,*
*   your young men will see visions.*
Even on my servants, both men and women,
*   I will pour out my Spirit in those days.'*
(Joel 2.28–29)

What a breathtaking prophetic picture! An outpouring on everyone!

This incredible image describes a vast deluge, wave, outburst and inundation of God's Holy Spirit. It is an expansive image of refreshing and overflowing life. We have become perhaps too familiar with the expression of an outpouring of the Spirit. Do we really consider its meaning, impact and consequences? God has promised to pour out the Spirit and he is able to do it. The Spirit of God wants to rush in to all our lives and communities.

This is something God has said he will do. We cannot engineer such an outpouring in our own strength. It comes from God. But, we can partner with God to see revival come. Only God can pour out his Spirit, but we can position ourselves ready and waiting for him to be faithful and fulfil his promises. God is sovereign, but we can lean into revival. We also have a responsibility to do all we can to promote such an outpouring of the Spirit in our lives, homes, churches and communities.

The promised Holy Spirit was first poured out on that Pentecost morning in Acts 2. That day, 3,000 people came to follow Jesus. The prayer gathering in the Upper Room overflowed with God's outpoured Spirit and the gospel went viral in Jerusalem. In his sermon that day Peter even quoted the Joel 2 scripture as being fulfilled. God's Spirit saturated the followers of Jesus and they were never the same again. Filled with holy boldness and fiery love, they shared the new message of Jesus with signs, wonders and miracles following. The Spirit was poured out and thousands of people came to faith in Jesus. Revival is when the gospel goes viral! That outpouring continues to this day and will continue until Jesus returns again in glory.

I believe the Joel 2 prophetic word absolutely applies to Pentecost, but it can also apply in our generation as well. We are still in that Pentecost season of the outpouring of the Spirit on the Church. Today, we are to plead the promise of Joel 2 over our cities, rural communities, towns, villages, neighbourhoods, homes, workplaces, High Streets, schools, hospitals, community centres and every-where else you can think of. I believe this is how local churches can change nations.

It starts by us depending on God in prayer just as they did in Acts 2; waiting for God's empowering presence. Praying for the outpouring of the Spirit, and believing in faith that God will move and answer our prayers. As Mike Pilavachi used to say so often at Soul Survivor summer festivals, 'The more we wait, the more he does.' The more we pray, wait, believe and expect from God, the more life the outpouring will bring.

Now is the time for us to be praying big prayers over our lives, families, churches and communities. We can pray prayers big enough to change nations. God is able to pour out his Spirit again on our entire land. I really believe this is God's heart. In 1 Timothy 2.4 we are reminded that God 'wants all people to be saved and to come to a knowledge of the truth'. The outpouring of the Spirit is for all who will come to Christ.

An outpouring for everyone

God is calling everybody! This is not just for some people, other people or special people. This move of the Spirit is for everyone who will come to Christ.

As a pastor, my heart is for absolutely everyone to know the saving, keeping and empowering love of Christ. I have often been perplexed that some people see themselves at the edge of church, when God sees no edges. With God there is no being on the edge. If we are in Christ, we belong to him as his people, pure and simple; united and beloved. Everyone who has come to Christ in repentance and faith is included.

God's house is for everyone. All who follow Jesus are at the centre of God's love, not on the edge. The question for us all is, 'What is my part in this kingdom adventure?' We all have a part to play and can grow in our churches a culture of ownership, responsibility, welcome, confidence, multiplication and care.

The gospel is for everyone. Jesus came for whosoever will come to him by repentance and faith. This means every person in every generation can be saved through Christ alone. The good news is for all. The Spirit can be outpoured anywhere and everywhere.

We need the Spirit to move in churches, homes, workplaces, public places and everyday places such as shops, neighbourhoods and streets. At a recent meeting for renewal in our church, one of our leaders had a prophetic word. He shared with me:

> I saw a group of what I can only describe as angelic beings on both sides of the church. One group above the balcony and another above the altar. They were holding what looked like large black cooking pots and they were filled with oil. It looked like they were waiting to be told when to pour the oil out as the pots tipped forwards at a slight angle.

I keep meditating on this picture of God getting ready to pour out his Spirit upon us. I pray, 'Lord, let it be today that the oil of your Spirit is poured out.'

As previously stated, our local church vision is for everyone: *Every Person, Every Place, Saturated with God*. It takes ALL of us together to live out our vision and values. We are not just a collection of individual Christians, but one family of God. The Christian life is lived with one another. The word 'everyone' appears over 50 times in the New Testament.

Colossians 1.28 says, 'He is the one we proclaim, admonishing and teaching everyone with all wisdom, so that we may present everyone fully mature in Christ.'[1] Everyone needs Jesus. Everyone deserves to hear the gospel. God wants everyone to be saved. The outpouring of the Spirit can touch anyone and everyone.

Saturated together

It is incredibly powerful that God calls us each by name as individuals, but also he calls us as one body, one bride, one community and one family: the Church. We are united with one another in Christ Jesus. We journey in being saturated in the Spirit together. We are never alone and we profoundly need one another. We need help, encouragement, support and courage in living in the power of the Spirit. This is described beautifully in Romans 12.9–16:

> Love must be sincere. Hate what is evil; cling to what is good. Be devoted to one another in love. Honour one another above yourselves. Never be lacking in zeal, but keep your spiritual fervour, serving the Lord. Be joyful in hope, patient in affliction, faithful in prayer. Share with the Lord's people who are in need. Practise hospitality. Bless those who

1 Other references include Luke 11.4, 10; John 13.35; 1 Corinthians 12.6; 2 Timothy 3.12.

persecute you; bless and do not curse. Rejoice with those
who rejoice; mourn with those who mourn. Live in harmony
with one another.

This is a high calling, but also costly. It takes loving sacrifice,
humility and selflessness and involves us all dying to self and
becoming more like Jesus. This journeying together comes from
encountering our Father God's great love and surrendering everything to him. Our surrender can often feel feeble and frail, but
God looks at our hearts and what matters most is that we keep
persevering in seeking his kingdom and keep in the flow of the
outpouring of the Spirit.

This was my encouragement in the letter I wrote to our church:

> Journeying together is both amazing and challenging. I believe
> as a church we have a deep desire to be more connected with
> one another, growing friendships and cultivating a sense
> of family. I also understand that for various reasons, some-
> times we can ebb and flow in terms of connection. Perhaps
> busy lives, complex commitments or other issues can lead us
> instead to quietly disconnect. My sincere invitation to us all
> is to connect with God and one another in a new and mean-
> ingful way. Seeing every person, every place saturated with
> God can only be done together. I am inviting us to be the
> change we want to see. Together, we are the church – every
> one of us can make a difference.

This is all about creating and keeping connection and care for
one another. It is important to be intentional about growing our
connection into the church body. I want to see everyone connected,
equipped and empowered to serve together.

Our churches need a fresh outpouring of unity, fellowship,
prayer, engagement, friendship, generosity and serving. Sadly,

many people in church see themselves as insignificant in some way. Perhaps not great at praying or evangelism. Let me say very clearly that every person is so significant. Every person is vital, included and needed for us to see the revival we long for.

As a pastor, I long that everyone may see how significant they are in God's purposes and for their local church. Your church needs you. The kingdom of God needs you. You are part of God's people and everyone is needed to pray, serve, go and love. God's people don't spectate; they engage.

This sense of eternal purpose and a sacrificial calling to unity fuels my commitment to my local church. I really notice when people in our church are absent. I really notice it spiritually. I don't think most people know the anointing they bring and how valued and needed they are in the gathered church community. I don't think they know what they carry spiritually and how important it is that we come together each week to encourage and serve one another. Most people think they won't be missed, but they really are, in a kind and healthy way. Everyone really matters in the church community.

My heart is to help people fully commit and engage with their local church. Commitment is really about love. Yet, it can be a struggle to generate a culture of prayer and deeper fellowship and to gain momentum when commitment is contested. It takes everyone making one another a key priority.

People may say, 'We want to pray,' but prayer meetings are neglected. They want deeper fellowship, but are too busy to meet with others. They want more mission, but outreach groups are small. We need to either repent of disobedience or change the wine-skin of church we have; perhaps both!

I believe this is a time to see a paradigm shift in understanding what it means to be a committed disciple and to belong to a church. Of course, there are good reasons for regular absences including health problems, reduced capacity, work patterns, wider family commitments and various other personal circumstances, and there must be generosity for such. However, for many people, we must simply embrace the cost of following Jesus, choose a steadfast commitment and learn to prioritise one another in a new and beautiful way.

I spoke recently with a missionary who has been working overseas for over 16 years and has now returned to the UK. She had really noticed a change in the UK Church concerning basic commitment and the dilution of a heart to serve. She noticed a Church which had become riddled with entitlements as people built their own 'little kingdoms' of money, career, family, house, car, holiday . . . and much more, rather than God's kingdom.

Sometimes we want God's power and to see great things, but are not prepared to simply put in commitment to God's kingdom and take spiritual responsibility for the need around us. Being saturated with God involves deep commitment as well as deep encounters.

Saturated in signs and wonders

Everyone who knows Jesus can also flow in the gifts and power of the Spirit. These signs and wonders are part of the outpouring of the Spirit on the Church, for the sake of the world. They are not toys, but tools for sharing the gospel and extending God's kingdom and glory.

Every local church can move in the supernatural power of God's kingdom. Spiritual gifts are given by the Holy Spirit, so they are available to every believer. The Bible is packed full of God's signs and wonders moving through ordinary people. Since our theme is being saturated, let's look at the miracles, signs and wonders involving water in the Old Testament:

- Noah's Ark (Gen. 6—9)
- The parting of the Red Sea (Exod. 14.19–31)

- Crossing the Jordan river (Josh. 3—4)
- Water coming from the rock (Num. 20.1–13)
- Naaman healed by dipping in the Jordan (this could also be read as 'plunged' or 'immersed') (2 Kings 5)
- Jonah rescued from the large fish (Jonah 1—2).

Now let's see the miracles Jesus did involving water:

- The transformation of water into wine at the wedding at Cana (John 2.1–11)
- The first miraculous catch of fish at the lake of Gennesaret (Luke 5.1–10)
- Healing at the pool at Bethesda (John 5.1–16)
- Calming of the storm on the Sea of Galilee (Matt. 8.23–27)
- Walking on water (Matt. 14.22–24).

Of course, there are many miracles not involving water, but as I reflected on the image of the outpouring of the Spirit, I thought it would be great to see some instances when the signs and wonders also actually involved water!

God wants to saturate us with supernatural power from heaven; the gifts, fruit and wisdom of the Spirit are freely available, by faith, to extend his kingdom, to everyone in his Church. That is part of God's plan for local churches to change nations.

Sadly, some people feel disconnected from this ministry in the power of the Spirit as something for everyday living. Perhaps it seems a bit strange, they don't know how to start or there is a lack of confidence to step out in obedience to God and simply pray for a sick person to be healed or ask God for a prophetic word for someone. To be honest, I feel like that most of the time. Most people don't walk around feeling super-confident; they feel super-weak. Ministering in the power of the Spirit is not about *us* feeling powerful, but about God being glorified and us stepping out with mustard-seed faith in *his* power. The ministry of the Spirit is not centred on us, but on God touching others through us.

It is so very important for the Church to recover the ministry of Jesus and step out in the power of the outpouring of the Spirit. This is what the world is waiting for. Christians practising what we believe and seeing miracles, healings, prophecies and deliverance happening in our communities. This ministry is for every church.

My own experience was one of initial scepticism, then a gradual realisation that the Bible does teach spiritual gifts are for today and the Spirit has given us gifts so we can share Jesus with power. I searched the Bible for myself and came to that clear conviction. But, it wasn't until I also stepped out in faith myself that I saw God move.

In 1992, I had seen God at work at Soul Survivor and New Wine, and had begun to believe God could do miracles. In 1993, I had the amazing first-time experience of leading someone to Christ and in 1995, I first spoke in tongues. It wasn't then until 2004 that I first saw someone healed having prayed for them. This happened in Sweden as I helped serve on a New Wine team. I prayed for a woman to be healed from deafness. To my amazement, her ear popped as I prayed in Jesus' name, and she could hear!

Having seen this happen, even though it was not the first time I had prayed with people, I wanted to see more. I wanted to see more people healed, so I stepped out more in praying for them. God was increasing my faith for healing.

Around this time, I also began to share prophetic words with people and began to learn how to prophesy and pray for the sick in line with Scripture. This was a moment of liberation for me as I had never really believed God's power would be outpoured to others through me. I learned as much as I could from others and from Scripture. I love to keep learning and growing in spiritual gifts.

Also, it may be helpful to say that I have not yet experienced healing myself from my very impaired eyesight, even though I have been prayed for so often. I have simply had to choose not to get offended that I have not yet been healed myself, and to keep serving others by praying for their healing.

Many of the people I pray for are not healed, but I want them all to know God's love as I pray for them. It is so important that people encounter God whether they are physically healed or not. I can't heal anyone. My responsibility is obedience to the Lord Jesus; so I pray for the sick and share prophetic words as I am led by the Spirit. I often feel weak as I do it, but it is part of the joy of flowing with the outpouring of the Spirit. Not I, but Christ!

There are helpful scriptural practices when praying with people, but there is no formula. This ministry of the Spirit comes from the overflow of the outpouring.

As Luke 4.18–19 says:

'The Spirit of the Lord is on me,
     because he has anointed me
     to proclaim good news to the poor.
He has sent me to proclaim freedom for the prisoners
     and recovery of sight for the blind,
to set the oppressed free,
     to proclaim the year of the Lord's favour.'

We need the fullness of the Spirit today so we can be saturated with signs and wonders. God wants people to experience his healing and saving power.

I have learned so much about ministering in the power of the Spirit through the New Wine movement. I love the gentle and supernatural ethos of New Wine in seeing kingdom ministry exercised by everyone. There are some fantastic resources available, such as John Coles' excellent book, *Learning to Heal* (2010), or Jordan Seng's very practical book, *Miracle Work* (2013). We can grow in this ministry and it is honestly such a joy. I love seeing people minister God's power in everyday situations. I love seeing people step out in such a way that only God can get the glory. We need more kingdom ministry flowing through every believer and every local church. Imagine the impact of signs and wonders breaking out across our nation.

In all this emphasis on God's power, we need to remember that God's most important gift is his love. That is why 1 Corinthians 13.1–8 declares:

> If I speak in the tongues of men or of angels, but do not have love, I am only a resounding gong or a clanging cymbal. If I have the gift of prophecy and can fathom all mysteries and all knowledge, and if I have a faith that can move mountains, but do not have love, I am nothing. If I give all I possess to the poor and give over my body to hardship that I may boast, but do not have love, I gain nothing. Love is patient, love is kind. It does not envy, it does not boast, it is not proud. It does not dishonour others, it is not self-seeking, it is not easily angered, it keeps no record of wrongs. Love does not delight in evil but rejoices with the truth. It always protects, always trusts, always hopes, always perseveres. Love never fails.

When the Holy Spirit saturates us and is outpoured among us, there are signs and wonders and demonstrations of God's wonderful power. Yet, above all else, there is also an outpouring of love, truth (John 14.17), faith (2 Cor. 4.13), grace (Heb. 10.29), holiness (Rom. 1.4), power (2 Tim. 1.7) and glory (1 Pet. 4.14). This is all part of everyone experiencing God's outpoured Spirit.

Being endued with power from on high (Luke 24.49) is not about how clever, well organised or advertised we are. It is about how anointed we are. If we are preaching, leading and living without the power of the Spirit, we are only playing. We really need the filling and power of the Spirit for effectiveness in prayer, justice for the poor, work, miracles, family life, marriage, leadership, parenting, singleness and everything else in life you can imagine. We need the help of the Holy Spirit.

Everyone is invited, included and empowered!

14

'When you pass through the waters': *embracing the cost*

'When you pass through the waters,
  I will be with you;
and when you pass through the rivers,
  they will not sweep over you.'
(Isaiah 43.2)

There is always a cost to revival that leads us to lean on Jesus. There is something profound about suffering that opens a door to experiencing the close presence of Jesus. This was the testimony of Isaiah's word of promise that the presence of God would be so real, even when the waters were high. The sweeping waters of suffering cannot overwhelm, because God says in that moment, 'I will be with you.'

Passing through the waters of adversity, pain, trial and sacrifice is only really possible because of the nearness and close companionship of God. Sometimes the trial is just part of living in this world, and sometimes it is a direct cost of following and being faithful to Jesus.

Seeking to live a God-saturated life is not easy. It involves robust surrender, cost, dying to self and it does not make us immune from the traumas and troubles of living in our broken world. We may experience deep waters of suffering through poor mental health, bereavement, loneliness, relationship problems or sickness. It can be tough to be a follower of Jesus in a dying world.

In Scripture, water also signifies these human struggles, cares and chaos. The Red Sea of the Exodus was a place of extreme difficulty transformed by God into a miraculous deliverance. When we follow Christ, we certainly encounter real-world griefs, trials and pains. True discipleship can be demanding, yet also fulfilling where we remain faithful to Christ no matter what it costs.

This is a place where 'deep calls to deep' (Ps. 42.7) and where there is profound testing and tangible sacrifice. Every revival is contested and, despite the wonderful fruit, there is also depth of cost and inconvenience. Isaiah 43 speaks of God's protection during passing 'through the waters', meaning the place of trouble and trial. How can we remain close to the Lord in such times of costly obedience?

Consider Peter walking on water to come to Jesus in Matthew 14.28–29. It took tremendous courage and was risky, but Jesus was there. Also, in Luke 8.22–25, Jesus calms the storm and the disciples are fearful they are going to drown. These were not friendly waters.

Look at how the psalm writers saw dangerous waters and the storms of life ready to overwhelm us:

He reached down from on high and took hold of me;
    he drew me out of deep waters.
(Psalm 18.16)

Save me, O God, for the waters have come up to my neck.
(Psalm 69.1)

Deep calls to deep in the roar of your waterfalls;
    all your waves and breakers have swept over me.
(Psalm 42.7)

Yet the Bible also beautifully paints a picture of God very much with us in deep waters. Even when we are going through testing times we can know refreshing, peace and the love of God. Look at these amazing scriptures:

As they pass through the Valley of Baka,
    they make it a place of springs;
    the autumn rains also cover it with pools.
(Psalm 84.6)

He makes me lie down in green pastures,
    he leads me beside quiet waters,
    he refreshes my soul.
(Psalm 23.2–3)

'But blessed is the one who trusts in the LORD,
    whose confidence is in him.
They will be like a tree planted by the water
    that sends out its roots by the stream.
It does not fear when heat comes;
    its leaves are always green.
It has no worries in a year of drought
    and never fails to bear fruit.'
(Jeremiah 17.7–8)

Many waters cannot quench love;
    rivers cannot sweep it away.
If one were to give
    all the wealth of one's house for love,
    it would be utterly scorned.
(Song of Songs 8.7)

Trials and troubles can lead us closer to Jesus if we open our hearts to him. Through hard times of every kind, God is calling us to yield all to him, to depend wholly upon him and to trust in him. When God's faithfulness meets our loving surrender, we discover intimacy with Jesus. Revival begins in this place of surrender. It is not easy or cheap. We struggle, and know it is costly. But, this is the reality of being transformed and renewed, not conformed to the world (Rom. 12.1–2).

Everything I am describing here is counter to the spirit of the world. Paul described it so well, saying, 'I have been crucified with Christ' (Gal. 2.20). This surrendering of ourselves and being a living sacrifice is foolishness to the world, but it is at the heart of embracing suffering for Jesus' sake.

Jesus has already surrendered his life. It's now our surrender that is needed. God is not withholding from us; it is often us withholding from him! This is the central call of the gospel: to deny ourselves, take up the cross and follow Jesus (Luke 9.23). Embracing the cost of revival and passing through the waters of suffering teaches us that most important lesson of all. It is not about me, it is about him. My life is for his glory.

Obedience, even through suffering, is God's one-step programme to joy. Roy Hession called the experience of this truth 'brokenness' in his classic book, *The Calvary Road*. He writes: '. . . the first thing we must learn is that our wills must be broken to His will.' He goes on:

The Lord Jesus cannot live in us fully and reveal Himself through us until the proud self within is broken. This simply means that the hard, unyielding self, which justifies itself, wants its own way, stands up for its rights and seeks its own glory, at last bows its head to God's will, admits it is wrong, gives up its own way to Jesus, surrenders its rights and discards its own glory – that the Lord Jesus might have all and be all.[1]

Jesus humbled himself even in suffering. We never see Jesus concerned with getting his own needs met first. What would the

---

1   R. Hession, *The Calvary Road* (London: CLC, 1974), p. 13.

martyrs say to us today as we assert ourselves and demand our rights? The trials call us to be humble, teachable, obedient and yielded to God. Our honour is to pick up the towel of servanthood, giving up our rights and allowing love for God, neighbour and ourselves to cause us to continually offer ourselves to God.

There is no pressure here. This is a surrender freely given, a love offering of ourselves. Surrender is by grace, not striving. A surrendered life is made perfect by God's grace. God takes my feeble surrender and makes it perfect by grace. Consider the incredible words of Scripture in 2 Corinthians 12.9:

'My grace is sufficient for you, for my power is made perfect in weakness.' Therefore I will boast all the more gladly about my weaknesses, so that Christ's power may rest on me.

Power made perfect in weakness

This really impacted me powerfully in December 2015 during a time of struggle in my own life. I was struggling with leading our church in a time when things felt overwhelming. I felt frustrated, despondent and deeply discouraged, even depressed. I felt it physically, like a weight on my body and soul. I was trying my best to lead and live for God, but felt as though I was just hitting a brick wall. I was really struggling.

I remember one day coming out into my vicarage garden. We have an amazing, large garden full of trees and nature. I stood there alone in the early winter garden which was not looking its best and all I could see was a mess. I was looking at a garden that had been beautiful some weeks ago. Some things I had planted then were still alive; others were now dead, or not as I had hoped they would be. Other plants had become very untidy and overgrown.

There were fallen leaves everywhere. I picked up a leaf and remembered that every leaf is created unique and beautiful, yet all

I could see was mess. I wanted to tidy it up and make it pristine again, but I couldn't do it. A garden is seasonal. It is sometimes tidy, other times messy. It is sometimes soggy or dry, sometimes there are weeds; sometimes I pull them up, then they just grow back. Sometimes the garden is exactly what you want it to be, other times it is a bit of a disappointment. Sometimes I need to prune and cut back or plant something in another place.

As I stood there in my frustration, I began to hear the Father's voice whispering to me: 'The church is a garden.' Then I remembered who the Gardener was in John 15; and it was not me! I just wanted to spend time in that garden with my good Father who is the Gardener. I realised my place was simply to abide and not be the Gardener.

As I reflected and listened some more I realised I was mistaking fruitfulness for orderliness. In church life, I was working hard making sure there were no weeds. But it is OK for a leaf to fall and for something to grow that I did not plant. I needed to be released not to be the Gardener, and simply to abide. I needed to stop stressing about trying to be the Gardener, and become a branch.

My Father is the Gardener. I could hear him speaking to me. Isn't the voice of God so amazing! As I prayed and reflected, I wrote, 'I want to hear Your voice and be restored into who You have called me to be, and not live under the weight of who I am not expected to be.' My dad was a farmer. I know that in farming and gardening you can't get perfection. Things will grow wonky and weeds will always grow, but my role was to abide and be fruitful. It's not about trying to be tidy and making everything perfect; it is about abiding in God's love. It means resting, loving, intimacy, time and listening to my Father's heart.

I reflected in my journal that day:

Maybe I have been stressing trying to tidy up and keeping things OK. I struggle when things are not OK. Trying to work it out, make it right, tidy it up. What is my Father's business in St Mary's? Do I believe God is at work? He called me to abide in Him and He would build the church, but I have taken it on myself to build, plan and get busy tidying up. Trying to make it the best I can. Father, please teach me to rest, listen and find quietness with God. Take from my soul the stress and anxiety. I want to be abiding in relationship. Show me the way not to be the farmer, but the branch. Teach me Your way. Abiding is intimacy and living beautifully. It is being saturated with God. Am I? Is the Vicar saturated? I am really a disciple, a branch, sent one, abider, a son, loved, Your child. I cannot fail because of Your love and sometimes I am much too busy. Thank You that You love me. You have been whispering this to me for a long time. Help me hear my Father speak. I want to be established in what You say. That is enough. Teach me, Lord. The church is a garden, not a factory. Our job is to abide; to slow down for connection with Jesus.

In John 15, Jesus' call to abide is all about our connection *with* God, not our activity *for* God. This coming to the end of ourselves and learning abiding is the secret of fruitfulness. Such surrender is not severe, it is a gift. As we offer our souls in our weakness, God can use us by grace and faith. Do I really believe without the Lord Jesus I can do nothing?

Our weakness exposes our hearts and shows us what we need to lay down. I had to lay down my fears of failure and my perfectionism so I could learn that even if I do nothing productive, I am utterly loved by God. I realised my fear of surrendering everything to God. I was fearful of others' opinions, yet longed to speak the truth in love. I realised that as a leader I felt responsible for everyone's happiness; I felt it was up to me to make the church grow and work for everyone. I was trying to please, bless and serve people, and of course not measuring up.

I was struggling to live up to my own values, to connect with God and people. I felt I was failing at the basics. I had a fear of people leaving our church and a feeling that I was letting people down. I felt a pressure to keep going and always be fresh. This all meant that my relationship with God was not intimate. I was drained by issues to which I did not have an answer. I was not caring for others well, or even myself.

My garden revelation was a key moment of God's nearness, kindness and help. The Church is a garden, not a factory. It is a beautiful mess and I am not the Gardener. My responsibility is to be saturated with God. I also wrote in my journal, 'I need to meet with God'; 'I am skimming and need to be saturated.'

There is such a profound connection between revival and our weakness. In Luke 1.37, Gabriel declares to teenage Mary: 'Nothing is impossible with God.' The power of God came upon her because of her utter dependency, not her capability. Mary was saturated with God, but not perfect and not strong. It's OK to struggle, and still be saturated.

Full and vulnerable surrender

Are we willing to pay the price and the cost of absolute surrender to Christ? Many are looking for fulfilment, but real joy comes through surrender. It is our surrender that God is looking for. I know what people mean when they pray, 'More, Lord' but I think our real need is not more of him. God has already given everything! He is not withholding anything. I think the prayer that God longs to hear is, 'Take, Lord.' More of my life yielded, offered, surrendered to you, Lord. Take my life.

What do I really mean by surrender? Let me put it as simply as I can:

- *Humility* – am I willing to humble myself? (1 Pet. 5.6)
- *Brokenness* – am I willing to bend my will to God's will? (Matt. 26.39)

- *Servanthood* – am I willing to become a servant? (2 Cor. 4.5)
- *Teachability* – am I willing to listen and obey? (2 Tim. 2.15)
- *Sacrifice* – am I willing to give up my rights? (1 Cor. 6.20)
- *Love* – am I willing to love God first, then my neighbour and myself? (Matt. 22.37–39).

Before we feel overwhelmed by our failure to live up to this, please remember that our surrender is imperfect. This is not about striving, perfectionism or pressure. This is where God's abundant grace comes in, making our vulnerable surrender perfect in God's sight. We don't make it perfect, God does, so we can boast in our weakness, yet still surrender all by grace.

The waters of testing, suffering, cost and sacrifice are there to lead us back to Jesus. Only when we are saturated in him can we face those other troubled waters. We need such resilient saints in this generation. People who have passed through the waters, saturated not with troubles, but with God.

Never thirst again!

My heart and prayer is that the new normal we all get to experience is revival.

Even in a dry and parched land where there is no water, there remains hope. The living water of Jesus brings new life, joy, laughter, freedom, meaning, wholeness and healing.

I want to close with two incredible scriptural promises and reflections.

Revival is a stream in the desert that is coming!

I love Psalm 126. As God restored Israel from captivity, it was described as being like a dream. It was almost too good to be true, but it happened! God did it. God keeps his promises and he is able, if we will prepare, get ready and turn to him.

We have not yet seen what God is about to do. He can do so much more than we have ever seen in this generation.

This was the psalm they sang on the first night of the Hebrides Revival:

> When the LORD restored the fortunes of Zion,
>   we were like those who dreamed.
> Our mouths were filled with laughter,
>   our tongues with songs of joy.
> Then it was said among the nations,
>   'The LORD has done great things for them.'
> The LORD has done great things for us,
>   and we are filled with joy.

Restore our fortunes, LORD,
    like streams in the Negev.
Those who sow with tears
    will reap with songs of joy.
Those who go out weeping,
    carrying seed to sow,
will return with songs of joy,
    carrying sheaves with them.
(Psalm 126)

I find the psalmist's description of moving from captivity to such freedom so compelling. The dream of seeing your community saturated with God. The transforming power of the God who 'has done great things for us'. People saved, strongholds broken, the sick healed, lost souls found, lives transformed, families reunited, crime falling, addictions broken, marriages restored, young people discipled; whole communities changed. This is revival!

May God give us such a song for our own day and our own land. May we see God at work in every person and in the midst of everyday life. Revival dreaming goes with revival weeping. Tears of compassion, honesty, conviction, desperation and intercession. Revival starts with dreaming and weeping in prayer. Bent knees, wet eyes and broken hearts. God, we need you, we miss you, we have wronged you, we want you.

Having seen just how parched our world is and how dry much of the western Church is, we definitely need the streams of the Spirit in the desert. This God-saturated psalm ends with a promise that those who weep 'will reap with songs of joy'. How we long for that time of incredible joy and breakthrough of harvest and the outpouring of the Spirit.

Our sincere prayer is found in the words of Isaiah 64.1: 'Oh, that you would rend the heavens and come down.'

And Psalm 85.6 is a prayer we can all pray often: 'Will you not revive us again, that your people may rejoice in you?'

May God get hold of us at last and may we see something different. Something that is missing, restored; something that is lost, found; something that is forgotten, remembered and experienced.

I have never seen the dry and parched land become saturated. I want to hear the sound and see the joy of a community saturated with God. Like Anna and Simeon, I want to see, hear and touch revival:

> LORD, I have heard of your fame;
>   I stand in awe of your deeds, LORD.
> Repeat them in our day,
>   in our time make them known;
>   in wrath remember mercy.
> (Habakkuk 3.2)

May God do something new, deeper and different. We do care about the missing revival. We want to see a fresh move of God that restores an awareness of him, an appetite for prayer and the anointing of the Spirit. More than that, God really cares! God longs to pour water on the thirsty ground. He longs to pour out his Spirit again on your community and this land.

You need never thirst again!

This is the ultimate promise for someone in a time of drought. You need never thirst again! Only Jesus can offer this confident guarantee.

In John 4.10–14, we find that Jesus is giving living water away to an ordinary, struggling and harassed woman from Samaria:

> Jesus answered her, 'If you knew the gift of God and who it
> is that asks you for a drink, you would have asked him and
> he would have given you living water.' 'Sir,' the woman said,

'you have nothing to draw with and the well is deep. Where can you get this living water? Are you greater than our father Jacob, who gave us the well and drank from it himself, as did also his sons and his livestock?' Jesus answered, 'Everyone who drinks this water will be thirsty again, but whoever drinks the water I give them will never thirst. Indeed, the water I give them will become in them a spring of water welling up to eternal life.'

Never thirst again! What astonishing hope! This is the opposite of being dehydrated. The opposite of the dry, parched spiritual lack we considered at the outset. Jesus really makes a courageous promise here of perpetual saturation. This is ongoing, uninterrupted, continual, persistent, unending access to living water. All from Jesus himself.

In this world we will thirst again, but the water of eternal life Jesus gives us means we will never spiritually thirst again! John also wrote about it:

'"Never again will they hunger;
   never again will they thirst.
The sun will not beat down on them,"
   nor any scorching heat.
For the Lamb at the centre of the throne
   will be their shepherd;
"he will lead them to springs of living water."
   "And God will wipe away every tear from their eyes."'
(Revelation 7.16–17)

Heaven will be the final resting place of no more thirst! It is the opposite of this dry, arid, sinful world. Jesus will give eternal life and endless living water to all who come to him by faith. So, we pray, 'Come, Lord Jesus.'

While we wait for that day of entire and eternal saturation in God, may we get as spiritually soaked as possible.

May we see the day at last when every person, in every place, is saturated with God.